AIR FORCE COLORS
VOL. I 1926-1942

by Dana Bell

illustrated by Don Greer
and Rob Stern

squadron/signal publications

ISBN 0-89747-091-5

For Doreen

The Mr. Jiggs emblem on the nose of this Martin B-12 identifies the 11th BS. The fuselage is glossy Olive Drab, while the wings and tail are Yellow. The propeller blades have been given a standard coat of Maroon antiglare paint. (USAF)

Acknowledgements

A history can be no better than its sources, and this book is no exception. Without the aid and assistance of a number of individuals and organizations, much of the information within these pages would not have been located.

Marilla B. Guptil of the National Archives, Modern Military Branch, was extremely helpful in discovering reports and correspondence in the Army Air Corps and Army Air Force files. Mr. Richard Thurm, of the Archives' Still Photo Branch, contributed his time in the search for photos in the 18-WP and 80-G files.

The National Air and Space Museum was a source of photos and countless details, and I am indebted to John M. Elliott, Robert C. Mikesh, and especially fellow Nutmegger Jay P. Spenser, for all their help.

Several offices within the Department of the Air Force helped in a variety of ways. Nancy Hogue of the Recognition Programs Branch, AFMPC, traced the records of several of the insignia shown in our color plates. Lt. Col. James L. Delaney of the Air National Guard History Office sent information on the National Guard units between the wars. David Schoem and Lawrence J. Paszek opened the files of the Air Force Office of History in Washington, D.C., and Jerry Hasslewander of the Albert F. Simpson Historical Research Center located a copy of Air Corps Board Study #42. Capt. Rick P. Du-Charme and Maj. Paul K. Kahl, Sr., of the Magazine and Book Branch, provided photos from the Air Force Still Photo Depository. The research staff of the Air Force Museum, in particular, Charles G. Worman, Ruth G. Hurt, and Patricia Turner were always there with encouragement and answers to my questions.

The Army's Institute of Heraldry was kind enough to provide a drawing of the insignia for the Command and Staff School, and the Defense Intelligence Agency provided photos from its files. Mr. Kenneth L. Kelly of the National Standards Institute gave access to vintage color specifications and samples, and helped interpret color differences.

Members of the International Plastic Modelers Society (IPMS), and the American Aviation Historical Society (AAHS), as well as a number of buffs and enthusiasts contributed in more ways than space permits me to describe. I owe a great deal to friends such as Peter M. Bowers, Robert Cressman, Arthur Eich, Roger A. Freeman, William Greenhalgh, Jr., Monty and Pat Groves (of Rarebirds), William T. Larkins, David Luccabaugh, James Maas, Ernie McDowell, David W. Menard, Joe Mizrahi (of Sentry Books), Mike Monaghan, Kenn C. Rust, Roy M. Stanley II, Paul C. Schmelzer, Osamu Tagaya, and Kenneth D. Wilson.

Upon learning of this project, Ross Whistler boxed two years of his own research materials, and shipped it via a well known national parcel delivery service. The package was lost in transit, with no hope of recovery. The loss of these records, representing so much hard work, is tragic. That it should happen to one as generous as Ross can only add to my personal regret. Many of the color equivalents at the back of this book are copied from his monograph "USAAF Camouflage, 1933-1969".

Robert L. Cavanagh went out of his way to help with this book. He contributed scores of photos and dozens of records, and put in many hours on the telephone, talking out the rough points. He proofread several sections of the text, adding many important details that had been overlooked. Bob's contributions have been so great, that if he had done much more, I would have had to list him as co-author!

Bruce Culver, Rob Stern, and Don Greer at Squadron/Signal Publications helped pull the finished product together, bringing up all the right questions and generally doing all the good things that publishers do. They somehow remained tolerant each time a deadline had to be extended, and were a great help whenever things jammed up. In particular, Don and Rob provided the excellent artwork on our color pages.

I would like to thank all of these individuals for their many contributions, and their support.

Finally, I must mention my wife Doreen, who has lived with this book longer than she may care to think about. She has helped in every aspect, from researching at the Archives on Saturday mornings, to typing captions, to rubbing my stiff back. She pushed when I needed pushing, and encouraged when I needed encouraging. She didn't even divorce me when I chained myself to the work bench for days at a time. And now that Volume I is complete, her only question is, "When is Volume II due?"

(A special thanks to J.C. for all his help, as always.)

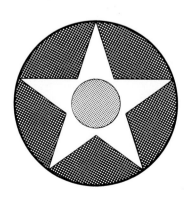

Introduction

This book begins a study of US Military aircraft color schemes from 1926 to the 1980s. The early years, from the post-WWI formation of the Army Air Corps to the establishment of a separate U.S. Air Force, were marked by phenomenal growth and development in all areas of aviation — all of which was reflected in changing markings and colors. A great deal has been written about this period elsewhere, but a brief overview may help the reader place details in their historical perspective.

In 1926, the Army Air Service was less than eight years out of World War I. Strength was about 9,700 officers and men (about one-twentieth of the wartime total) in thirty-two combat squadrons. The tactical force in the continental United States was organized under the 1st Pursuit Group, 2nd Bombardment Group, 3rd Attack Group, and 9th Observation Group, with an independent observation squadron assigned to each Army corps. Overseas squadrons were formed into composite groups, of which there were three (the 4th Composite Group in the Philippines, the 5th in Hawaii, and the 6th in Panama). Curtiss P-1's, Boeing PW-9's and Douglas O-2's were beginning their service careers, but the majority of aircraft in inventory were older designs, such as the Curtiss Jennies and American-built DH-4's.

There had been many bright spots in the years since the War. Airpower had been established in the public eye by such events as the sinking of the captured German battleship Ostfriesland in 1921, the non-stop, coast to coast flight of a Fokker T-2 in 1923, and the round-the-world flight of a pair of Douglas World Cruisers in 1924. But 1925 had ended with the court-martial of Colonel William "Billy" Mitchell, former Assistant Chief of the Air Service, and outspoken proponent of military aviation. Mitchell's criticism of his superiors in the Navy and War Departments did much to bring what he described as, "the incompetency, the criminal negligence, and the almost treasonable administration of our national defense" to public attention, but his statements were to cause his own downfall.

On July 2, 1926, Congress passed the Air Corps Act, creating the Army Air Corps and beginning a five-year modernization program. New units were to be activated, new aircraft purchased, and personnel strength increased to over 16,500 men and officers. But the basic organization, a sore point with Mitchell and his followers, remained unchanged. The Air Corps was to be a logistical and training organization, just as the Air Service had been. Tactical training of combat units, and operations were the responsibilities of the various ground force commanders to whom these units were assigned. While much had been written about aerial armadas that could strike deeply at an enemy's industrial heart, doctrines of the day placed aviation in support of the armies, much like some form of flying artillery or a mobile observation post.

The next five years were to see a great deal of shifting, as combat squadrons were reorganized into training units, and then reorganized again to form new combat groups. By 1932, the Air Corps had reached its goal of fifteen tactical groups.

In March, 1935, the General Headquarters Air Force (GHQAF) was formed to centralize tactical control of all domestic pursuit, bombardment, and attack units. This organization was separate from the Air Corps, which continued to be responsible for personnel training and logistics. It was not until June, 1941 that the Air Corps and Air Force Combat Command (a redesignation of GHQAF) combined to form the Army Air Forces.

Although rearmament was well under way, the USAAF was not prepared when War came that December. By June of 1942, Japanese expansion had been checked in the Pacific, but the Navy's victory at Midway, the turning point in that theatre, required little effort from the AF. The Solomons Campaign had not yet begun, nor had American air operations in Europe and the Middle East. The color schemes and markings of these campaigns, through the end of the war to the establishment of the US Air Force will be the subject of Volume II of this series. Certain other schemes, which were in limited use before June of '42, will also be covered in Volume II. (These schemes include sea search, haze paint, and night camouflage.)

The correlations between Air Corps history and aircraft color schemes can take many forms. The need for a radio call designator for an aircraft without a radio was as unlikely as the need for a natural metal finish on a fabric-covered plane. Similarly, early organizational markings emphasized the squadron or flight, as these were the basic units to a flying formation. By the time 1,000 plane raids became common, wing and division markings predominated. Budgetary considerations, particularly during the lean years of the Depression, brought about many economy finishes, such as the unpainted metal of the late '30s.

A good deal of information is available from regulations, general orders, technical orders, and specifications of the period, though a certain caution must be exercised in their use. This particularly applies to dates of publications: it might require years for a change to become effective in all units, or a change may be published to legalize a practice that had been widespread for months. Unit markings, generated at the air base level, are more difficult to trace. Coverage of all the markings of groups and squadrons would be beyond the scope of this volume, although an attempt has been made to include as many as possible. Insignia drawings are included in the color section, but again, these are not inclusive. Numerous unofficial emblems were common, as were minor variations of the basic designs. Also, units were often redesignated, retaining the original insignia. This was particularly true of attack units, which all were redesignated as bombardment units in 1939, and pursuit units, which became fighter units in May of 1942.

American cities were not laid siege during the Second World War. Public records and archives were not captured or sacked, and yet, surprisingly little documentation remains to explain the colors of this period. Every effort has been made to locate remaining files, but there is still a great deal missing from the picture. Someday, a cache of records may be found, not unlike a warehouse full of Africa Corps pith helmets, but until then, this book may serve as a primer.

"…. a red circle inside of a white, five-pointed star inside of a blue circumscribed circle. The circumference of the inner circle shall be tangent to the lines forming a pentagon made by connecting the inner points of the star." (ORDERS No. 20, Director of the Air Service, May 17, 1919.)

Standard Insignia, Markings and Colors

Army aircraft markings and colors were prescribed by a series of technical orders, specifications, and standards. These publications regulated sizes, locations, and colors of markings, as well as materials to be used and methods of application. A newly manufactured airplane, or one being returned from overhaul at a depot, was expected to have these standards applied, leaving unit markings as a local responsibility.

The national markings in early 1926 were four star-insignia placed on wings, with three vertical stripes on the rudder. The star-insignia began to replace the red, white and blue World War I style three-circle insignia (cockades) in May, 1919. Although it required several years to completely change all aircraft, by 1926 all the three-circle wing markings were probably gone.

The vertical rudder stripes had seen several arrangements during the Great War, but since that time the standard had been: blue at the rudder post, followed by white and then by red. This marking was soon to pass, however. New rudder stripes, recommended by Charles N. Monteith, a Boeing Seattle engineer, were approved by the Secretary of War in November 1926, and specifications were amended in January, 1927. The revised markings used a vertical blue stripe at the rudder post, followed by seven red and six white horizontal stripes.

The original colors of the insignia were required to match colors of the American flag: white, ultramarine blue and venetian red. Sometime between 1926 and 1928 these colors were altered to a darker blue and red, with white. Dates and reasons for the change are unknown at this writing.

The rudder carried an additional marking, the aircraft model designation and manufacturer (e.g. Curtiss PW-9C), in small black letters. This spanned older 'three-stripe' rudders (about one third of the way from the top), and was carried within the upper white stripes for rudders of the new design.

Every Army aircraft was identified by a serial number, and this was painted in 4 inch high digits, just forward of the stabilizer. A number of aircraft continued to carry old style serials, almost as high as the depth of the fuselage side but these numbers eventually were replaced or the aircraft left service. Serials were required to be white unless against light blackgrounds, but black numbers were actually quite common on dark fuselages.

In February, 1924, station commanders were given the option of having 'U.S. Army' painted under wings and on fuselages to distinguish Air Service aircraft from those of other departments, commercial concerns, or individuals. This became mandatory for all Air Corps aircraft under a Technical Order dated 15 October 1926. 24 inch letters below the wings and four inch letters on the fuselage were to be black or white, whichever best contrasted the background color.

Numerous other standard markings were used, generally covering the requirements and cautions involved in servicing or repairing the aircraft. Dope codes (usually visible on the rudder) carried information describing the date and type of finish applied. Strut numbers were used to identify struts by location. A data block near the cockpit listed instructions on fuels, weights, and loading. Also, numerous smaller markings noted hand holds, fire extinguisher locations, warnings, etc.

The standard color for Army aircraft was Olive Drab (O.D.) overall: top, bottom, wings, fuselage — anywhere not covered by a marking or insignia. When freshly doped, this color was actually quite glossy, but exposure to the elements tended to matt this somewhat.

The O.D. scheme, while not overly conspicuous, was not considered a camouflage. During WWI the U.S. was developing camouflage schemes for its aircraft, but the Advanced Section of the American Expeditionary Forces recommended against this. Despite colorful national markings, Allied aviators had frequently shot at each other, confusing all camouflaged aircraft for German machines. The British chose to paint their aircraft overall khaki, and the Americans followed suit. As it was for vehicles and equipment, Olive Drab was simply the "Army color" for airplanes.

The P-12E "TIGER" on page 40 carried yellow diamonds on the cowling, yellow stars on wheels, and red horizontal tail surfaces.

To increase visibility of aircraft that might be forced down in uninhabited regions particularly foreign countries or territorial possessions, station commanders were allowed to apply yellow paint to the top surface of upper wings. This began early in 1924, about the same time yellow was first applied to U.S. Navy aircraft, though records do not indicate that a joint decision was made. When, in 1927, the color was standardized for all Army aircraft, it was to be painted on all wing and tail surfaces. (The Navy evidently thought little of this idea, and generally limited its use of yellow to the top of the upper wing).

The Air Corps Act of 1926 brought about an increase in training activities. Because of the relatively low visibility of the standard Olive Drab paint, there was a marked increase in training accidents, especially mid-air collisions. It was obvious that a new high-visibility scheme was needed for trainers.

Tests of suitable paint colors for trainers were conducted in 1927-1928. Light Blue was chosen over silver and was then applied to all trainers during overhauls.

This Boeing built DH-4M-1 over Hawaii in October 1926 carries an Olive Drab fuselage with Yellow upper wing and vertical tail. Sixty inch diameter insignia are placed tangent to the wing tips, overlapping the ailerons. The three vertical rudder stripes were standard until early November. (USAF)

"F.A.I.D." is listed as manufacturer on the rudder of this Thomas-Morse MB-3M, reflecting the fact that the aircraft was rebuilt at Fairfield Air Intermediate Depot. Olive Drab overall, 43rd School Squadron, Kelly Field, Texas. April 1926. (USAF)

The prescribed rudder insignia for Air Service aircraft was:
3 equally wide bands, red, white and blue, and both sides of that portion of the rudder which are in the rear of the rudder post shall be striped parallel to the vertical axis of the airplane. The blue band shall be nearest the rudder post, the white band in the center, and the red band at the tail of the rudder ...

(War Dept. Orders No. 20, May 17, 1919)

Revised rudder striping was approved by the War Department in November, 1926. The technical description, as published the following January, read:
a. Design. — The insignia on the rudder shall consist of one blue stripe parallel to the rudder post and thirteen alternate red and white stripes parallel to the longitudinal axis of the airplane ...
b. Blue Stripe. — The width of the blue stripe shall be ⅓ of the maximum width of the rudder within the normal contour of the rudder to the rear of the fin.
c. Red and White Stripes. — The portion to the rear of the blue stripe shall be divided into thirteen stripes parallel to the longitudinal axis of the airplane. The location of these stripes shall be determined by dividing the distance between the highest and lowest point on the rudder to the rear of the blue stripe into thirteen equal parts. There shall be seven red and six white stripes.
d. Location. — The rudder insignia shall be placed on that portion of the rudder to the rear of the fin. Balanced portions of the rudders which extend forward over or into the fin shall be finished the same color as the fin surfaces.

(quoted from Spec. 98-24102K, November 1, 1935)

Paragraph 'd' was to have particularly important implications when the rudder post was located aft of the rudder's leading edge. On aircraft such as the O-19 and B-18, this placed the stripes part way back on the rudder.

A Curtiss P-1B shows its underwing markings during acrobatics over the Nation's Capital in 1927. "U.S. Army" is in two foot high white letters beneath the Olive Drab wing, as standardized in October 1926. (USAF)

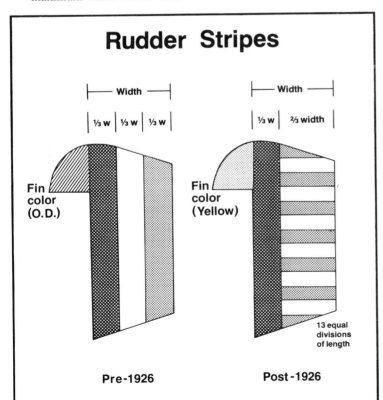

Rudder Stripes

Pre-1926

├ Width ┤

│ ⅓ w │ ⅓ w │ ⅓ w │

Fin color (O.D.)

Post-1926

├ Width ┤

│ ⅓ w │ ⅔ width │

Fin color (Yellow)

13 equal divisions of length

(Above) *San Antonio,* one of the six Loening OA-1A Amphibians in the 1926 goodwill tour of South America, rests on the beach at Montevideo. Fuselages and wingtip floats were black, but all wing and tail surfaces were painted yellow to increase visibility in event of a forced landing. (USAF)

The Yellow wings of these 7th Observation Squadron DH-4s are clearly visible over the jungles of Panama. Application of the Yellow dope was limited to the upper surface of the top wing and the vertical tail. 1927 (USAF)

This pair of Olive Drab Curtiss NBS-1s was photographed during the Air Service Maneuvers of Spring 1926. In the foreground the 2nd BG insignia and black-yellow-black stripe (the group colors) mark an aircraft of the group headquarters section. The other bomber is assigned to the 96th BS with that squadron's insignia and red-black-red fuselage band. (USAF)

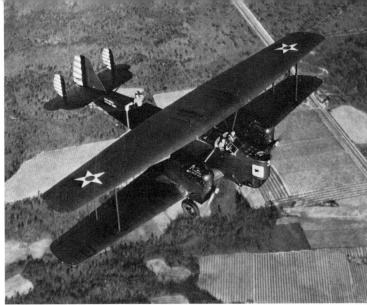

Parachute jumping at Brooks Field, Texas, in 1927. The aircraft are Atlantic (Fokker) DH-4M-2Ts. Apparently, a recent overhaul included the painting of revised rudder stripes, smaller wing insignia and the relocation of the manufacturer's name and aircraft type to the rear fuselage. (Author's Collection)

For tapered wings, such as this Keystone LB-5 (s/n 27-337), the wing stars were positioned a distance one-eighth of the wingspan from the wing tip, tangent to the aileron. The 20th BS's pirate is painted on the nose. (USAF)

The prescribed location of the "star insignia", as published in Orders No. 20, May 1919, was:

> ... the upper and lower surfaces, respectively, of the upper and lower planes of each wing in such position that the circumference of the circle shall be tangent to the outer tips of the planes. One point of each star shall be pointed directly forward and unless otherwise specified, an insignia diameter of 60 inches shall be used for most wings. (An "otherwise specified" diameter was required for wing chords of less than 60 inches; in these cases the diameter usually equaled the chord.)

In January 1926, the following changes to the size and location of wing star insignia were published in Spec 98-24102:

> Size of Insignia for Airplane Wings. — For wings the diameter of the circumscribed circle shall be ¾ of the available chord length at the location specified. The available chord length is the whole chord on wings not having ailerons, and is the chord length from the cut-out for the aileron to the leading edge on wings having ailerons. Where the wing covering is both fabric and metal, the available chord length shall be that portion of the metal-covered portion only.

> Fore and Aft Location on Airplane Wings:
> a. Wings with Aileron. — The insignia shall be located tangent to the cut-out for the aileron on wings having ailerons.
> b. Wings Less Aileron — The center of the insignia shall be located midway of the chord on wings not having ailerons.
> c. The insignia shall be located on the metal covering tangent to the joint between the metal and fabric covering on wings where both fabric and metal are used for the wing covering.

> Lateral Location on Airplane Wings:
> a. The center of the insignia shall be located in from the wing tip a distance equal to 1/16 of the wing span on wings not tapered, and distance equal to 1/8 of the wing span on tapered wings.
> b. When meeting the requirements of this specification, the outside edge of the circumscribed circle comes closer than six inches to the wing tip, the insignia shall be moved inboard to bring the outside edge of the circumscribed circle six inches in from the wing tip.

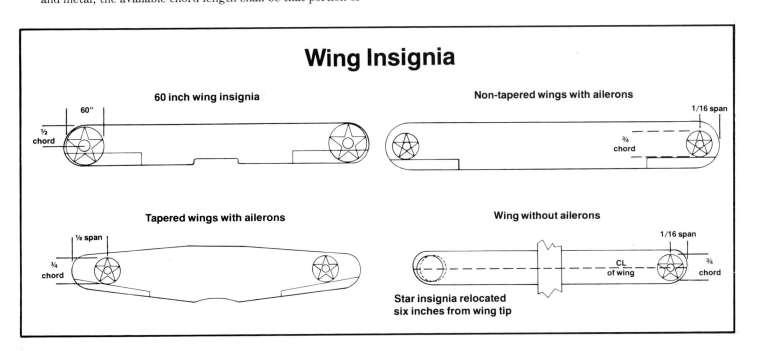

Wing Insignia

60 inch wing insignia

60″
½ chord

Non-tapered wings with ailerons

1/16 span
¾ chord

Tapered wings with ailerons

⅛ span
¾ chord

Wing without ailerons

1/16 span
CL of wing
¾ chord

Star insignia relocated six inches from wing tip

This factory fresh Curtiss A-3 Falcon carries the identification markings that became standard for Army aircraft in 1926. The manufacturer and type designation are on the rudder, and "U.S. Army" has been added to the fuselage above the Air Corps serial number. (USAF)

Frequent replacement of fabric made the rudder an inconvenient location for the type designation and manufacturer's name. Rather than continually repaint these markings the Air Corps ordered them located beneath the serial. 91st Obs. Squadron. (Authority: T.O. 1-1-16, 18 October 1927). (USAF)

A common feature of markings of the 1920s was the technical data block seen here below the cockpit of a Boeing P-12B. The majority of this information was moved to technical manuals in the early 1930s. (USAF)

In 1929, the serial block was reorganized with the manufacturer and aircraft type as the middle line. (Authority: Spec. 98-24105L, 25 January 1929). This aircraft is assigned to the 94th PS whose Indian head insignia can be seen on the bright red ring cowl. (USAF)

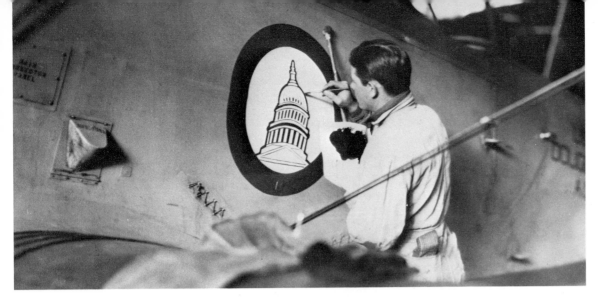

Unit Markings

The practice of distinguishing between units with colors or designs predates the airplane by thousands of years. The spear ornaments of the Persian Immortals, the cap devices of warring Scottish clans, the shield patterns of the Zulu nation, and the striking falcon of the 27th Pursuit Squadron have served the same purpose: differentiating between various military bodies, fostering a fighting spirit within these units, and organizing them during the chaos of battle.

The Aeronautical Division established the 1st Aero Squadron during the Mexican Punitive Expedition in 1913, but the only "unit" markings were large aircraft numbers on the fuselage. World War I brought an increase in the number of units, and the introduction of distinctive unit markings. Although styles changed over the years, the same three types of marking were used on nearly all military aircraft: organizational insignia, unit recognition devices, and individual recognition markings.

The organizational insignia were emblems or shields, usually placed somewhere on the fuselage. In 1924, these became subject to War Department approval, and many of the WWI designs were eliminated for a variety of reasons. (The 94th P.S. 'Hat in the Ring' for example, was dropped rather than provide an advertisement for Rickenbacker automobiles.) Though there were exceptions, it was not common for a squadron to change approved insignia, even though redesignation would make a design obsolete — the 48th Pursuit Squadron emblem is an example, having been approved for the 48th School Squadron, the preceding designation.

A design submitted for approval was expected to be simple, usually depicting something of historical significance to the organization, capable of being reproduced by relatively unskilled personnel, and distinguishable at a distance of at least 150 yards. The layout could not include numerals, the letters 'U.S.', the Air Corps insignia, the U.S. flag, any part of the U.S. coat of arms, the complete coat of arms of any state or country, outlines of geographic maps, foreign decorations (e.g. Croix de Guerre, Victoria Cross) or campaign ribbons. Additionally, policy statements periodically banned designs that implied death, the devil, destruction, or games of chance, in spite of the fact that all were in use by at least one unit at any given time.

The plight of the 21st Pursuit Squadron is one illustration. In a period of eighteen months, this organization carried three different emblems, with only one achieving official approval. The initial design, submitted in May, 1940, was an Ace Of Spades (symbolizing death) and Jack of Spades (cunning, shrewdness, and initiative); together, a winning hand in '21', with a thunderhead and bolt of lightning in the background (symbolic of sudden, deadly power from the sky). This was rejected in July, for stressing "the destructive nature of warfare".

The 21st's commander resubmitted the design that December, but changed his description — perhaps an act of cunning, shrewdness,

and initiative on his part! Now, the Ace of Spades became a symbol of "Fate", and the thunderbolt represented "force and aerial activity". The rejection in January, 1941, was to comply with a War Department policy which deemed "symbols representative of games of chance" inappropriate.

The third attempt at approval made no changes, and was rejected in August, 1941. That same month, a new emblem was submitted, based on a bee named "Battlin' Buzz", but this was considered too similar to the 43rd P.S. emblem, and rejected.

The final insignia of the 21st Pursuit Squadron was approved in November, 1941, and is shown in the color drawings on page 40. The American Indian (representing "courage and daring") and tomahawk (for "Tomahawk" equipment — the 21st had just re-equipped with P-40's) met all standards. The final irony was only weeks away — the 21st would be battered by the initial Japanese attacks on the Philippines, with only a handful of aircraft on hand by the end of the year.

Unit recognition markings could be designed and revised with more freedom, usually needing only the approval of the group commander concerned. One pattern was usually selected for the entire group, and applied in the colors of each of the group's squadrons, or in the colors of the group headquarters section. It should be noted that, prior to 1937, each group and squadron had its own heraldic colors. These colors were the basis for the unit's recognition markings and were often incorporated into the unit emblem.

The purpose of this type of marking was to provide an immediate recognition feature that could be identified at the limits of insignia visibility. Any design, from a discrete band on the cowling or tail to a wild flash arching across the fuselage, was considered appropriate.

Individual recognition markings were also the responsibility of the unit commander. Each aircraft within a group was assigned an individual identification number. This was originally painted on the fuselage, but was relocated on the tail by most units about 1930. Contrary to popular belief, these numbers were not related to aircraft serial numbers. It appears that only the 1st Pursuit Group and 3rd Attack Group used the last two digits of the aircraft serials as individual numbers, and then only during the early 1930s.

Special aircraft, such as those of group, squadron, or flight commanders were often assigned symbols such as chevrons, diamonds or stripes to aid in rapid recognition of these individuals.

Unit applied markings were often changed, and few records were kept. This, coupled with the indifferent quality of black and white photos has left a maze for modelers and historians who attempt to unravel the markings of the period.

Another common marking of the period was a city or state name, which was often assigned to an aircraft during a special christening ceremony. All such names were ordered removed in January, 1936.

(Above) The nose and forward engine nacelles made popular locations for displays of squadron colors. The 11th BS used these sawtooth flashes for its aircraft, Curtiss B-2 Condors. (USAF)

Even a quick glance will point out the variations in the hand painted snow owls of these 17th PS P-6Es. National Air Races, 1932. (USAF)

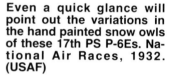

This Curtiss O-1E wears the insignia of Air Corps Detachment, Bolling Field in Washington, D.C. The state name and arrow on the nose were common practice for this unit, which was often known as the Bolling Field Detachment. The nose is yellow. (USAF)

The 90th AS was equipped with Curtiss A-3s from 1930 through 1934. The Squadron colors of red and white are used for the aircraft number on the fuselage, the nose trim and the wheel hubs. (USAF)

When the 6th PS decided to change its distinctive insignia, this unauthorized pterodactyl was carried on the fuselage. Rejection of the design by higher headquarters forced the return of the more familiar skull within a spinning prop as emblem. (AFM via Cavanagh)

The 13th AS was a sister squadron to the 90th AS and used blue and white squadron colors in the same fashion. Yellow wings and tail appear darker due to the use of orthochromatic film, which lightens blue and darkens red and yellow. (USAF)

National Guard Observation squadron insignia often derived from divisional insignia of units to which they were attached. This 119th Obs. Squadron (New Jersey NG) O-2H carries the insignia of the 44th Infantry Division. (USAF)

A Thomas-Morse O-19E of the 22nd Obs. Squadron. Note the red cowl ring and nose flash, barely visible in this print made from an orthochromatic negative. (Bowers via Cavanagh)

The Fokker C-2A "Question Mark" made one of the most famous endurance flights in history. The Bolling Field Detachment insignia and a large white "?" are carried on the fuselage with the number 51 in black on the tail. The refueling aircraft is a Douglas C-1. January 4, 1929. (USAF)

Before aircraft radios were standard equipment, important messages were often whitewashed onto a convenient aircraft fuselage and "air mailed". This PW-9 served in that capacity during the "Question Mark" endurance flight. (USAF)

One of the earliest examples of personal artwork painted on an Air Corps aircraft is carried on this A-3 in 1929. Note the early form of the 3rd Attack Group insignia bolted beside the gunner's cockpit. (USAF)

Little is known about markings used to identify Flights within Squadrons. In this well known photo of the 27th PS's P-12Es, half of the aircraft have noticeably darker vertical tails, apparently in Flight colors. (USAF)

Flight identification colors are easily distinguished on the tails of these Curtiss B-2 Condors. The lead V appears to be the squadron C.O. and his wing men. The 2nd V is probably A Flight leader and his two wing men. (USAF)

In 1931, Air Corps depots were assigned arrowhead insignia. This O-25A was used for photographic purposes at Wright Field and has that organization's blue and gold arrowhead between the wings. (USAF)

The insignia of many of the Air Corps schools were often carried on a white rectangular background. This is the case with this Y1C-14 assigned to the Air Corps Technical School. (USAF)

The 88th Obs. Squadron used its orange and black squadron colors on a diagonal fuselage band as well as the nose and engine nacelles. Shown here is a Fokker O-27. Notice the Navy-style red, yellow and blue propeller tips. (Menard via Cavanagh)

This Curtiss P-1D was assigned to (then) Major Clarence L. Tinker in May 1930 while he was an instructor at Kelly Field. The insignia of the 10th School Group is on the tail with the 43rd School Squadron insignia and the legend "Celito Lindo Mexico" between the wings. "Pathfinder" is painted above the exhaust stacks. (AFM via R. L. Cavanagh)

In 1931, the First Pursuit Group was granted permission to display the group insignia as well as individual squadron insignia. Here the group markings are displayed on the tail of a 17th P.S. Curtiss P-6E Hawk. (via Cavanagh)

Unit insignia often included plants and animals found near the home base. The 24th PS in Panama adopted the Jaguar as can be seen on this pranged PW-9C in August, 1929. (via Cavanagh)

Another aircraft assigned to the Panama Dept., this OA-1A has the 7th Obs. Squadron's emblem below the pilot's front cockpit. The aircraft is painted aluminum with yellow wings and tail and black antifouling paint below the water line. Seven, the aircraft number is repeated on the fuselage, upper wing and wing tip floats. (via Cavanagh)

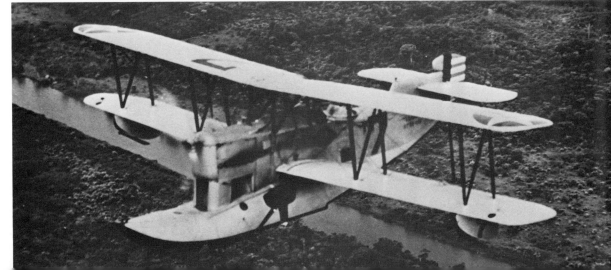

The 17th Pursuit Group on the line at March field. The first two aircraft are assigned to the group headquarters section, and are marked with the group colors of red and yellow. Aircraft "00" wears the markings of the 1st Pursuit Wing. (USAF)

Squadrons within a group usually wore similar markings but in respective squadron colors. 17th Pursuit Group generally wore fuselage blazes with scalloped tails, headrests and wheel pants. This P-26 uses the black and white colors that identified the 34th PS. (USAF)

73rd Squadron colors were red and yellow. For identification from below, the squadron number was painted beneath the fuselage, just behind the wing. (USAF)

95th PS colors were blue and yellow (reversed for contrast when blue fuselages were introduced). All of these "Peashooters" had OD fuselages with yellow wings. Note that the 95th PS did not repeat the aircraft number on the fuselage spine. (USAF)

Air Mail

The Army Air Corps Mail Operation (AACMO) of 1934 was a disaster which served only to bring the Air Corps' weaknesses in to the public view. When the President cancelled Contract Air Mail Service in February, 1934, alleging collusion between the U.S. Post Office and the air transport industry, the Army was expected to assume control of a system that had been carefully developed since 1926. After sixty-six accidents, and the loss of twelve lives, in less than 3½ months, this embarassing chapter was closed on 1 June. Arguments for the reorganization and strengthening of the Air Corps received the most effective boost possible, short of war.

Two views of 12th Obs. Squadron O-35s during the air mail emergency. Aircraft assigned to a particular air mail route often carried the route number in addition to normal unit markings. (USAF)

The Army made limited use of overall white for some of its ambulance aircraft. The single Y1C-15 built shows standard markings with the addition of a large red cross on each side of the fuselage. (USAF)

A high visibility scheme developed on the O-2H and K in 1928 substituted Light Blue for Olive Drab on the fuselage. Many of these aircraft served in the basic training role, including this O-2H at Kelly Field, Texas in 1932. The serial data formerly painted on the rear fuselage is just visible above the technical data block. (USAF)

A number of commercial transports were accepted with unpainted aluminum skin in the late 1920s. The 90th Attack Squadron used this Ford C-9 trimotor as a hack during winter maneuvers in January, 1930. (Nils Arne Nilsson via McDowell)

The majority of trainers wore OD fuselages, standard for all Army aircraft of the 1920s. This PT-1 was photographed during maneuvers in September, 1929. (Kercher/AFM via Cavanagh)

The Air Corps experimented briefly with aluminum doped fuselages for primary trainers during the late 1920s, apparently comparing the visibility with light blue. It is interesting that the same scheme, including yellow for all wing surfaces, was delivered on similar Consolidated aircraft used by the Navy. (USAF)

The high visibility blue/yellow scheme appears to have been successful enough to cause the repainting of all Air Corps trainers. Specific instructions to this effect have not been found among Air Corps records, but the change probably started in 1929 or 1930. The School of Aviation Medicine operated this PT-3A in April, 1932. (USAF)

Major General J.E. Fechet served as Chief of the Air Corps from 14 December 1927 until 19 December 1931. He was photographed in the rear cockpit of this O-1C, two days before assuming office. The fuselage is probably glossy black. (AFM via Cavanagh)

Fechet's successor as Chief of the Air Corps, Major General Benjamin D. Foulois can be noted in the crowd beside his Douglas O-2D. The aircraft appears to have a deep blue fuselage with silver wings and tail. (USAF)

VIP Aircraft

The small number of aircraft refitted for special duties as staff transports were usually reserved for high ranking officers and civilian officials within the Air Corps. Modifications often included a second set of controls; at least one machine had a washstand so that the Chief of the Air Corps could clean-up after a long trip.

The most visible external change was in color scheme and markings. Glossy Black and Dark Blue fuselages were common, and in some cases, the wings and tails were silver rather than yellow. The authority and origin for these schemes is unknown, and although the colors may have been a matter of personal choice, specific directives have been located for parallel schemes on Navy aircraft. Even the aircraft which bore standard color schemes usually displayed special markings (such as general's rank or office emblems).

There are indications that a number of group commanders carried dark blue fuselages on their aircraft, even though this practice is hard to prove.

The flag of the Assistant Secretary of War for Air is mounted just ahead of the Bolling Field Detachment insignia of this C-4A trimotor. 'Oklahoma' the aircraft name is on the nose. (USAF)

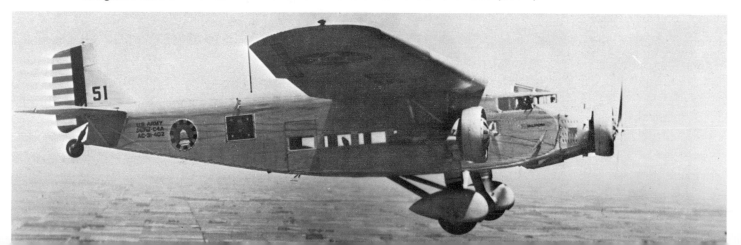

Curtiss A-12 Shrike, 26th Attack Squadron, Hawaii, 1936. (USAF)

Blue Fuselages

The use of two separate color schemes, Light Blue for trainers, and Olive Drab for tactical aircraft, caused logistical headaches for Air Corps maintenance facilities. Quantities of O.D. and Light Blue paints were required in stock at all times. Another problem was the need to know an aircraft's ultimate destination before paint could be applied: examples of many aircraft served in training roles, and thus required blue fuselages.

The solution, as recommended by the Chief of the Materiel Division in January 1934, was to standardize one paint scheme for all aircraft, regardless of role. His choice was Light Blue fuselages with Yellow wings and tails, reasoning that high visibility was essential for trainers, while temporary water paint camouflages made the lower-contrast Olive Drab for tactical aircraft unnecessary. Stocks of Olive Drab were at the reorder point, making a timely decision that much more important, and in February the recommendation was approved

by Chief of the Air Corps. Revised specifications and T.O.'s were printed in May, and shortly afterward, tactical aircraft were noted with Light Blue fuselages.

Overnight repainting of the entire inventory was not suggested, and certainly did not occur; the added burden on depots would have proven far too expensive. Instead, as aircraft went through periodic depot overhaul, old paint was replaced with fresh coats of Light Blue. It took several years for the process to be completed.

Black and white photos give the impression that several hues of Light Blue were being applied by the Air Corps. Although several shades of Light Blue were used, they did not vary as much as photographs would indicate. Tonal shifts of contemporary films are the root of the confusion; the two standard films of the day either lightened (Orthochromatic) or darkened (Panchromatic) any blues photographed. Light Blue appears so dark on Pan. film that it is often difficult to tell from Olive Drab.

Misinterpretation of black and white photos may have led to the contention that a light green paint was used by the Air Corps in the mid-'30s. Certainly, records of this period do not support this, and those fuselages alleged to be light green were probably light blue.

First ordered in Fiscal Year 1934, all Martin B-10B's were delivered from the factory with Light Blue fuselages. This 9th BG formation is led by three red, white, and blue cowled aircraft of the 1st BS. (USAF)

P-12B engine change in the field. Once again, pan film gives the illusion of a darker fuselage. Insignia is for the 36th P.S., July, 1935. (USAF)

This Boeing P-12C or D carries the Army's Command and Staff School insignia. The wheel and cowling checks are blue and yellow. (via Cavanagh)

Ortho film accentuates the fading and bleaching of this 1st Observation Squadron O-1G. (via Cavanagh)

COLOR FOR ARMY AIR CORPS AIRPLANES
Specification No. 98-24113
May 23, 1934

Ailerons - both surfaces	Yellow No. 4	Skis. No added finish	
Cowling - external surfaces	Light Blue No. 23	Spinners	Light Blue No. 23
Elevators - both surfaces	Yellow No. 4	Stabilizers, both surfaces	Yellow No. 4
Fins - both surfaces	Yellow No. 4	Struts, landing gear	Light Blue No. 23
Flaps - both surfaces	Yellow No. 4	Struts, wing	Light Blue No. 23
Floats, Wing - above water line	Light Blue No. 23	Struts, wire braces	Light Blue No. 23
Floats, Wing - below water line	Black.....	Struts, fairing	Light Blue No. 23
Floats, Wing - water line stripe one inch wide	Yellow No. 4	Step plates	Black.....
Fuselage	Light Blue No. 23	Tail Wheel Fork	Light Blue No. 23
Fuselage, Wing Fairing	Light Blue No. 23	Walkways	Black.....
Horns - Color of surface to which attached		Wings, both surfaces	Yellow No. 4
Hulls - above water line	Light Blue No. 23	Wheel Cowling	Light Blue No. 23
Hulls - below water line	Black.....		
Hulls - Water line stripe two inches wide	Yellow No. 4		
Propeller Blade - flat surface when required	Maroon No. 18		
Propeller - No finish on other surfaces	.....		
Rudders, balanced portion - both surfaces	Yellow No. 4		
Rudders, rear of post (See Specification No. 98-24102)			

Special accessories which must not be used for hand-holds shall be finished in aluminum, natural cadmium plating, or natural polished metal. These include pitot-venturi tubes, radio masts, radio loops, and venturi tubes.

A blue fuselaged Consolidated PB-2A with markings of the Headquarters Section 1st Pursuit Group. May, 1937 (USAF)

An O-25C of the 16th Observation Squadron. Nose trim and fuselage stripe appear to be red with white borders. (via Bob Cavanagh)

In a novel approach to drag reduction, the Bellanca C-27 used a combination wing strut/airfoil to brace the top wing. This was Yellow and carried 'U.S. Army' in black, as if the lower wing to a biplane, but all national insignia were applied to the main wing. Struts and wheel pants were Light Blue, as was the fuselage. (USAF)

This Douglas OA-3 has the standard scheme for amphibians in 1935. The fuselage above the water line, and engines were painted similar to any other aircraft. The areas below the water level are Black, with a Yellow stripe at the water line. Markings are for the 4th Recon Obs. Squadron with a Red two star General's flag on the tail. (USAF)

National Guard markings replace 'U.S. Army' beneath the wing of these 118th Obs. Sq. O-46As. These markings were common from December, 1928 until just before the war. (USAF)

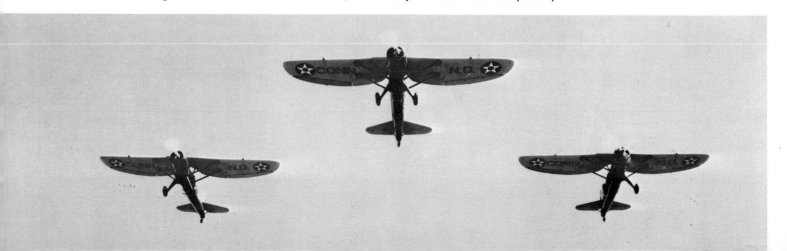

The Squadron emblem resembling a dinosaur's head is the hornet's nest of the 3rd Air Base Squadron. The guns have been removed from this P-6E, which serves as unit hack. (NASM)

Loading ammo for a P-26's 30 caliber guns. In the early 1930's, the data panel was removed from aircraft leaving the aircraft type, serial, and crew weight. Aircraft were normally assigned to fields rather than units and the field name was often painted above the serial block. (USAF)

(Below) Out to pasture? This derelict P-12, formerly of the 6th PS, has been staked out for target practice near Bellows Field, Hawaii in October, 1937. The flash on the forward fuselage is red and white. (USAF)

Aluminum Finish

Before examining the decision to use aluminum finish for Air Corps aircraft, a few words on the protective qualities of paints are in order.

Dope painted onto fabric surfaces tightens, shrinks and hardens the skin, providing strength not found in unpainted fabric. Dope also waterproofs, an essential quality for any aircraft that might fly through rain; imagine a linen wing that absorbed moisture, gaining weight and sagging like a wet beach towel! Lastly, dope protects the fabric from rot.

Lacquers and oil based enamels are the two most common paints for metal surfaces. Aluminum alloy skin possesses inherent surface strength, regardless of paint coatings, and does not absorb moisture. Corrosion and oxidation are legitimate problems, however. The danger is not as obvious as rusted steel on an old car. Rather, an aluminum wing is destroyed by intergranular corrosion, which is almost invisible.

The Air Corps' first experience with an unpainted all metal aircraft involved the Ford XC-3 Trimotor. The corrugated aluminum alloy sheet covering this aircraft was coated with an electrochemical film (in a process known as anodizing) to inhibit oxidation. In 1932, after 1,300 hours flight time and four years service, a depot inspection turned up minute grayish-black spots on the wing surface. Further testing revealed that intergranular corrosion had set in, and the integrity of the wing had been destroyed.

The 1934 inspection of another Ford Trimotor (a C-9) found no fatigue or corrosion problems, despite the nearly identical service records of the two aircraft. Both were built from the same grade aluminum alloy, but the C-9 had been coated with 1½% pure aluminum. Thus treated, the sheeting (known as "Alclad") was able to resist scratching and offer superior protection for relatively minor weight increases.

Numbers of metal covered aircraft were entering service in the early 1930s, and specially finished alloys, such as Alclad, enabled them to be operated without external paint. The reason for switching to a "natural metal" finish was entirely economic. Weight savings were actually minor in 1934, only about 25 pounds for a pursuit ship, and close to 80 pounds for a bomber. The real savings were to come in overhaul time and dollars. A depot overhaul required between 175 and 400 hours to remove old paint in order to check for skin fatigue. Refinishing required an average of $250 per airframe. In March, 1935, the Air Corps approved plans to take advantage of unpainted metal tactical aircraft, only to be delayed by yet another economic consideration: supplies of Light Blue and Yellow paint, stocked the previous autumn, had to be used before a new scheme could be adopted. Unpainted tactical aircraft would not be accepted from manufacturers until 1937 and Technical Orders for aircraft in service were not changed until March 1938.

Blue and Yellow remained standard for trainers and amphibians, due to the need for high visibility on these aircraft. The wings of tactical aircraft were often painted yellow if there was additional danger of forced landings, over such locations as Panama or Alaska.

Fabric covered aircraft acting in a tactical role, or fabric covered portions of metal aircraft, were to be doped aluminum, to achieve uniformity with metal aircraft. Older metal types without special coatings were inspected regularly for tell-tale signs of corrosion, and many were simply painted with aluminum paint. Anti-glare panels ahead of cockpits and inside engine nacelles were commonly painted Flat Bronze Green 9, rather than flat black, until August, 1942, when a new color — Dull Dark Green — was introduced.

A highly-polished Douglas C-39 banks into the afternoon sun. The aircraft is assigned to the Sacramento Air Depot. September 1939. (USAF)

Varying grades of aluminum give this Michigan Air National Guard O-47 a patchwork effect. The antiglare panel ahead of the cockpit was flat Bronze Green. (Paul C. Schmelzer)

Not natural metal, but aluminum paint — the Martin B-10B required additional protection for its aluminum alloy skin. The tail surfaces appear to be Yellow. 28th BS, Philippines, November, 1939. (USAF)

One of the four O-49s modified for ambulance duties. This aluminum doped Stinson carries a permanent red cross on the fuselage. Moffett Field, California, 6 December, 1941. (William T. Larkins)

This Y1A-18 was assigned to the 8th Attack Squadron. The squadron insignia is chalked on the fuselage but not yet painted in. The cowlings, however, are yellow, the squadron color. Sept., 1937. (USAF)

Another 3rd Attack Group aircraft, this time a 90th AS A-17A, showing the "E" marking on the tail. The squadron color is red. November, 1937. (USAF)

Use of the letter 'E' on the vertical fin by the Air Corps is often attributed to aircraft in an "experimental" or "evaluation" status. The difficulty with this presumption is the continued use of the letter long after aircraft have been accepted into service use, such as in the 1937 photo of an 8th Attack Squadron A-17A, shown above.

In fact, the letter 'E' was awarded annually during squadron competition at Barksdale Field, Louisiana. The award, known as the M. F. Harmon Efficiency Trophy, was presented to the 90th A S in 1937, the 79th P S in 1938, and the 8th A S in 1939. The marking was removed each year as a new squadron took top honors. (An earlier Navy practice was to award the 'E' on an individual basis.) The designators described on pages 31 and 32 left little room on the fin, so the 79th P S wore its 'Es' painted on the cowling.

Identification of the letter 'B' carried by several bomb units is not yet certain, but it is reasonable to expect that something similar to the Harmon Trophy was in use for an annual bombing competition.

The 'B' below the 96th BS insignia on the Y-1B-17 was probably awarded for excellence in bombardment, a practice usually associated with the Navy. The black area below the nose is an anti-glare panel around the bombardier's window. (USAF)

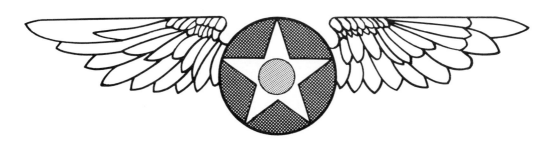

GHQAF and the Designator System

Advocated since the days of General William 'Billy' Mitchell, the General Headquarters Air Force (GHQAF) came into being in March 1935. For the first time since the Great War, the striking and air defense forces were placed under the command of a single air officer, rather than being broken up for piecemeal employment by various ground commanders. All of the pursuit, bombardment, and attack units in the U.S., as well as 6 of the domestic observation squadrons, were organized under three wings. However, the majority of observation squadrons, as well as all the combat air units in Panama, Hawaii, and the Philippines remained under the control of the respective ground commanders. Also, training, depot, and a score of miscellaneous functions stayed under the control of the Air Corps — which remained a separate organization, linked in no way to the GHQAF! That the Chief of the Air Corps and the Commanding General of the GHQAF reported separately to the Army's Chief of Staff was to create serious coordination problems for years. Although no longer tied to individual divisions or corps, the combat air arm could no more control the design of its aircraft than it could specify a new howitzer for the field artillery.

Externally, the most visible change came on 15 November 1937, with the first coordinated system for aircraft markings and call letters. Previously, unit identification markings had been subject to the whims of each group commander, and they could change just as often!

This left a legacy of interesting color schemes, though many resist interpretation today.

Use of squadron and group insignia was unchanged, covered by the same tech order applying to Air Corps aircraft, but the employment of squadron colors and command markings was standardized, and a new system of airplane markings, known as designators, was introduced.

White, yellow, and red became the only specified squadron colors for most pursuit, attack, and bombardment units, although a fourth squadron attached to a group was to be assigned the color blue. "A suitable depth of the front portion of engine nacelles", as called for in the order, allowed some latitude in the application of these colors, but eliminated the use of long fuselage flashes and scalloped tails. The more colorful designs of the early thirties were giving way to order. In 1940, three-squadron groups were given their choice of any of the four squadron colors.

Cowlings for group headquarters squadrons were divided into sections using the colors of each squadron in the group, while reconnaissance squadrons were assigned color combinations by respective wing commanders. Reconnaissance squadrons were not organized into groups; in the GHQAF, these squadrons were assigned directly to a wing. The wing headquarters themselves, as well as air base squadrons and GHQAF command aircraft, were not allowed recognition colors, eliminating the possibility of a variety of elaborate schemes in these units.

Command markings also were overhauled, with a series of fuselage stripes replacing the chevrons, diamonds, and random bands of earlier days. These five inch stripes were to be in the squadron color, with black replacing white on aluminum fuselages, and white replacing blue on blue fuselages. Although group commander stripes were never prescribed, several units employed fuselage stripes of each of the squadron colors for this purpose.

Staff aircraft of GHQAF and the Air Corps. The A-17A above wears the winged star of the GHQAF. Below, an A-17 AS (three-seat modification), wears the 'Capital Dome' of the 14th BG, which absorbed the Bolling Field Detachment and its insignia in spring, 1935. (NASM and Schmelzer)

B-17s of the 2nd BG on the line in 1938. Aircraft #51 wears squadron commander stripes in black on the rear fuselage. (USAF)

The most innovative change was the designator; marked on the tail and above and below the left wing, it identified the unit of an aircraft even if the unit insignia could not be seen or recognized. Generally, the first letter indicated the type of unit and the second letter gave the number of that unit, with a number to identify the individual aircraft within that unit. Thus, the number 58 aircraft of 1st Pursuit Group became P (for Pursuit) A (first letter of the alphabet for the First Group) 58. The radio call letters, formed from the letter 'G' and the designator, would then be "GPA-58".

It was common for a three squadron group to reserve the numbers 1 through 9 for the headquarters section, with other squadrons in the group being assigned number blocks of 10-39, 40-69, or 70-99 (The squadron C.O. generally took the highest or lowest number of his block.) In the few cases where a squadron was assigned more than thirty airplanes, numbers from similar blocks in the one-hundreds range were used (e.g., 110-139 for a squadron with the block 10-39). Generally, these airplane numbers bore little relation to the serial number. These numbers were usually black on light colored tails and yellow on most dark surfaces.

The GHQAF standard for designators and aircraft markings was used until mid-1940, when it was modified for use by all units of the Air Corps as well. Curiously, some units in the Hawaiian and Panama Departments adopted similar markings to the GHQ system in 1939, although it is not known if this was due to an Air Corps directive — or just the whim of the group commanders!

HQ 1, etc.	Headquarters, GHQAF
WA 1, etc.	1st Wing
WB 1, etc.	2nd Wing
WC 1, etc.	3rd Wing
AC 1, etc.	3rd Attack Group
AQ 1, etc.	17th Attack Group
BB 1, etc.	2nd Bombardment Group
BG 1, etc.	7th Bombardment Group
BI 1, etc.	9th Bombardment Group
BS 1, etc.	19th Bombardment Group
PA 1, etc.	1st Pursuit Group
PH 1, etc.	8th Pursuit Group (incl. 37th A.S.)
PT 1, etc.	20th Pursuit Group
KA 1, etc.	1st Air Base Squadron
KB 1, etc.	2nd Air Base Squadron
KC 1, etc.	3rd Air Base Squadron
KD 1, etc.	4th Air Base Squadron
KE 1, etc.	5th Air Base Squadron
KF 1, etc.	6th Air Base Squadron
R 1 thru 15	18th Reconnaissance Squadron
R 16 thru 30	21st Reconnaissance Squadron
R 31 thru 45	38th Reconnaissance Squadron
R 46 thru 60	41st Reconnaissance Squadron
R 61 thru 75	88th Reconnaissance Squadron
R 76 thru 90	89th Reconnaissance Squadron

HQ designators mark an A-17A, and in the background, a B-18. Many B-18s were converted for a transport role. (NASM)

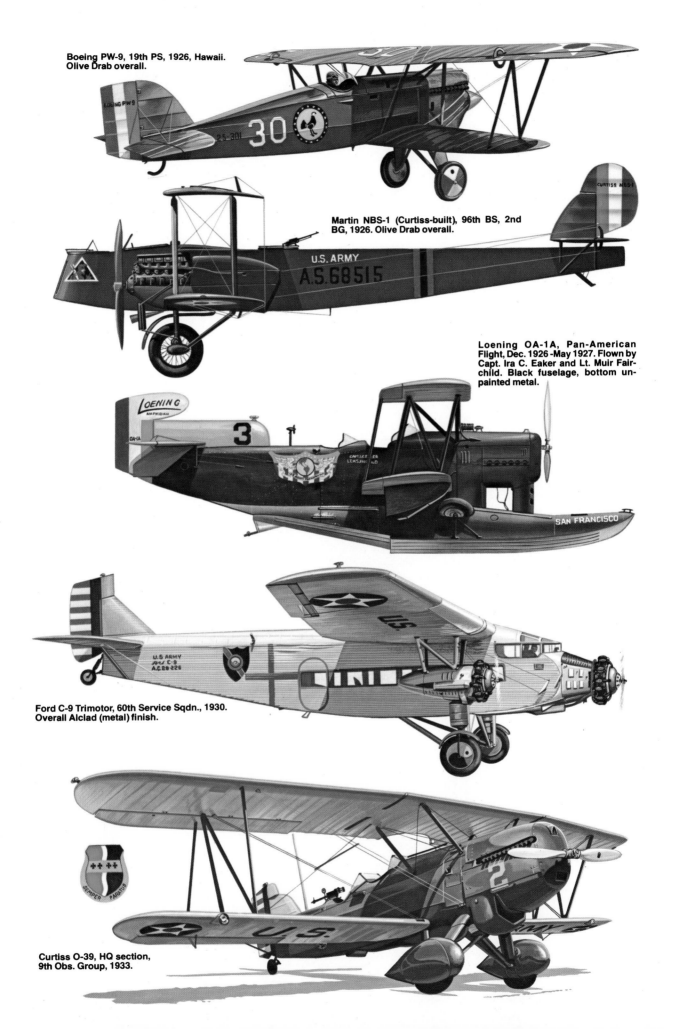

Boeing PW-9, 19th PS, 1926, Hawaii.
Olive Drab overall.

Martin NBS-1 (Curtiss-built), 96th BS, 2nd
BG, 1926. Olive Drab overall.

Loening OA-1A, Pan-American
Flight, Dec. 1926 -May 1927. Flown by
Capt. Ira C. Eaker and Lt. Muir Fair-
child. Black fuselage, bottom unpainted metal.

Ford C-9 Trimotor, 60th Service Sqdn., 1930.
Overall Alclad (metal) finish.

Curtiss O-39, HQ section,
9th Obs. Group, 1933.

The black fuselage band on this 17th PS P-35 marks the B flight leader's aircraft. Although the squadron color is white, command markings are in black, for greater contrast with the aluminum skin. (Paul C. Schmelzer)

Flight Officers of the 1938 Good Will Flight to Buenos Aires are photographed in front of a 2nd Bomb Group B-17. This Headquarters Squadron plane has each cowling in a different permutation of the squadron colors. (The young navigator on the right would one day be Air Force Chief of Staff: Lt. Curtis E. LeMay). (USAF)

Command Bands

Squadron Commander

'A' Flight Leader

'B' Flight Leader

'C' Flight Leader

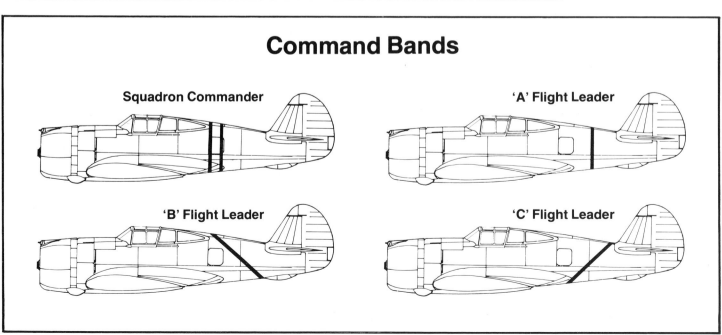

The 21st Recon Squadron flew B-18s from 1937 to 1941. The squadron color, probably red, is used on the cowlings and the 'A' Flight Leader fuselage stripe. (USAF)

B-18s of the 7th BG at March Field in 1940. Note the B (for bombing excellence?) on the nose. (USAF)

"R 34" is the squadron commander of the 38th Recon. Squadron. Both the cowlings and the squadron leader stripes have a yellow and black checked design. BS-1 is assigned to the Headquarter section 19th Bomb Group and has its cowlings quartered in red, white, blue and yellow. (USAF)

Curtiss P-6E, 17th PS, 1st PG, 1932.
1st PG insigne on rudder.

Curtiss P-1B, 27th PS, 1930.

Combat Groups

1st Purs   **2nd Bomb**   **3rd Attack**   **4th Comp**   **5th Comp**   **6th Comp**

7th Obs   **8th Purs**   **9th Bomb**   **10th Trans**   **11th Bomb**   **12th Bomb**

13th Bomb   **14th Purs**   **15th Purs**   **16th Purs**   **17th Bomb**   **18th Purs**

19th Bomb   **20th Purs**   **22nd Bomb**   **23rd Comp**   **25th Bomb**   **27th Bomb**

28th Bomb   **29th Bomb**   **31st Purs**   **33rd Purs**   **34th Bomb**   **35th Purs**

36th Purs   **37th Purs**   **40th Bomb**   **42nd Bomb**   **43rd Bomb**   **45th Bomb**

48th Purs   **50th Purs**   **51st Purs**   **55th Purs**   **56th Purs**

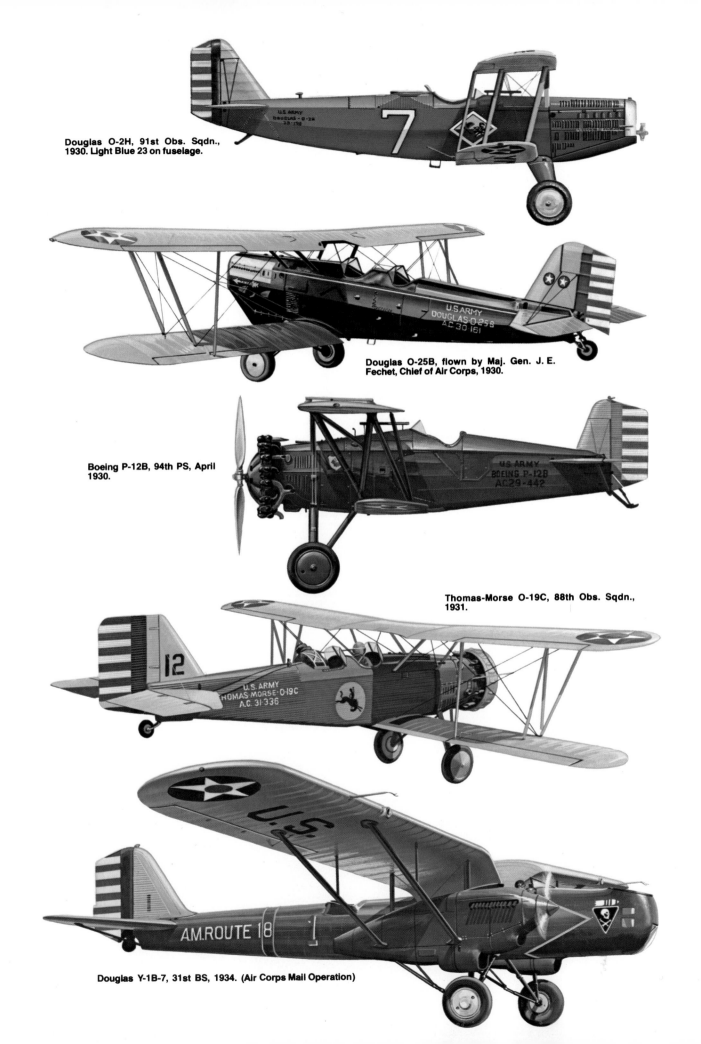

Douglas O-2H, 91st Obs. Sqdn.,
1930. Light Blue 23 on fuselage.

Douglas O-25B, flown by Maj. Gen. J. E.
Fechet, Chief of Air Corps, 1930.

Boeing P-12B, 94th PS, April
1930.

Thomas-Morse O-19C, 88th Obs. Sqdn.,
1931.

Douglas Y-1B-7, 31st BS, 1934. (Air Corps Mail Operation)

The crest of the 17th Attack Group is barely discernible above the camera window of this Vultee A-19. (via Cavanagh)

The designator below the left wing was generally placed anywhere there was room, as can be seen from these 1st Pursuit Group ships. The location of the word "Army" was usually the deciding factor. (Paul C. Schemelzer)

A blue and yellow BC-1 of the 3rd Air Base Squadron. The location of the designator above the left wing is unusual. (NASM)

A 4th Air Base Squadron C-33, with typical markings for support units in 1938: the designator and blue/gold squadron insignia are the only additions to the factory scheme. (USAF)

Although the 18th PG was not part of GHQAF, its aircraft wore designators as early as 1939. These Hawaii based P-26s are with the 19th PS (NASM)

Boeing P-12E, 24th PS, Panama, 1934.

Squadron Insignia

1st Bomb

1st Obs

1st Recon

2nd Bomb

2nd Obs

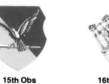

2nd Recon

2nd Trans

3rd Bomb

3rd Purs

3rd Obs

4th Bomb

4th Obs

5th Obs

6th Bomb

6th Purs

6th Trans

7th Bomb

7th Obs

8th Attack

9th Bomb

10th Recon

10th Bomb

11th Bomb

11th Recon

12th Obs

12th Recon

13th Attack

14th Bomb

15th Bomb

15th Obs

16th Obs

17th Bomb

17th Purs

18th Bomb

18th Obs

19th Recon

19th Bomb

19th Purs

20th Bomb

21st Purs

21st Recon

22nd Obs

23rd Bomb

24th Purs

25th Bomb

26th Bomb

27th Purs

28th Bomb

29th Bomb

29th Purs

Squadron Insignia

30th Bomb   31st Bomb   32nd Bomb   33rd Purs   33rd Bomb

34th Attack   35th Bomb   35th Purs   36th Purs   37th Bomb   37th Purs

38th Purs   38th Recon   39th Bomb   39th Obs   39th Obs   39th Purs

40th Attack   40th Bomb   41st Purs   41st Recon   42nd Bomb   43rd Bomb

43rd Purs   44th Recon   44th Bomb   44th Purs   45th Bomb   46th Purs

48th Bomb   48th Purs   49th Bomb   50th Purs   50th Obs   52nd Bomb

54th Bomb   55th Purs   56th Bomb   60th Purs   61st Bomb   63rd Bomb

65th Purs   66th Purs   69th Purs   70th Bomb   70th Purs   72nd Bomb

73rd Attack   74th Attack   77th Purs   78th Purs   79th Purs   81st Bomb

82nd Bomb   82nd Obs   88th Obs   89th Obs   90th Attack   91st Obs

93rd Bomb   94th Purs   95th Bomb   96th Bomb   97th Obs   99th Bomb

The three pursuit squadrons of the 20th Pursuit Group share the group designator (PT). The P-36s represent, from left to right, the 77th PS (squadron color red), 55th PS (blue, changed from white for improved contrast), and the 79th PS (yellow). January, 1940. (USAF)

In 1939, Air Corps attack units were redesignated as light bomb units. All but one of these 3rd Bomb Group (Light) Y1A-18s have had their designators repainted as the year comes to a close. Squadron colors are yellow for the 8th BS and blue for the 13th BS (USAF)

20th PG Boeing P-26s were unusual in that *all* aircraft in the group wore the group crest, not the respective squadron insignia. Reasons for this anomaly are unknown. (USAF)

A pair of B-17s display both styles of aircraft designators. In the foreground, a 7th BG B-17C marked "7B 52" flies with a 19th BG B-17B coded "BS 35". January, 1941. (USAF)

Revised Designators

Two major changes took place within the designator system in May, 1940. New designators were added, so that every active flying unit in GHQAF *and* the Air Corps would be assigned a code. And individual organizations were identified by unit number, rather than a corresponding letter. The major reason for the second change was the 41 Group Program of May 1940. In Spring, 1939, the Army had hoped to ready 24 Tactical Groups by the end of June, 1941, (the 24 Group Program), which conveniently fit the 26 letters of the English alphabet; the 41 Group Program provided 15 more groups than the alphabet did letters. The new designators were painted in the same location as the GHQAF designators had been, although the unit was now placed above the aircraft number rather than below it.

National Guard Observation Squadrons did not carry an Θ in their designators, since all National Guard squadrons were serving in the observation role. Traditionally, these squadrons were numbered between 100 and 199, but the hundreds digit was dropped in the interest of brevity. If a Guard unit was "called up" or activated, the designator was changed to one appropriate for an observation unit, including the hundreds digit. Thus the 4th aircraft of the 115th Observation Squadron carried the designator 15 NG 4 when serving with the Guard, or 115 Θ 4 when activated.

Composite groups used two letters; the first was 'M' for miscellaneous unit, and the second indicated the mission of the squadron, such as 'B' for a bombardment squadron within the group.

Two O-46As a world apart. On the left, a squadron hack for one of the pursuit squadrons of the 4th Composite Group, Philippine Islands, 1941. On the right, the 119th Obs. Squadron, New Jersey National Guard. (Bob Cavanagh; USAF)

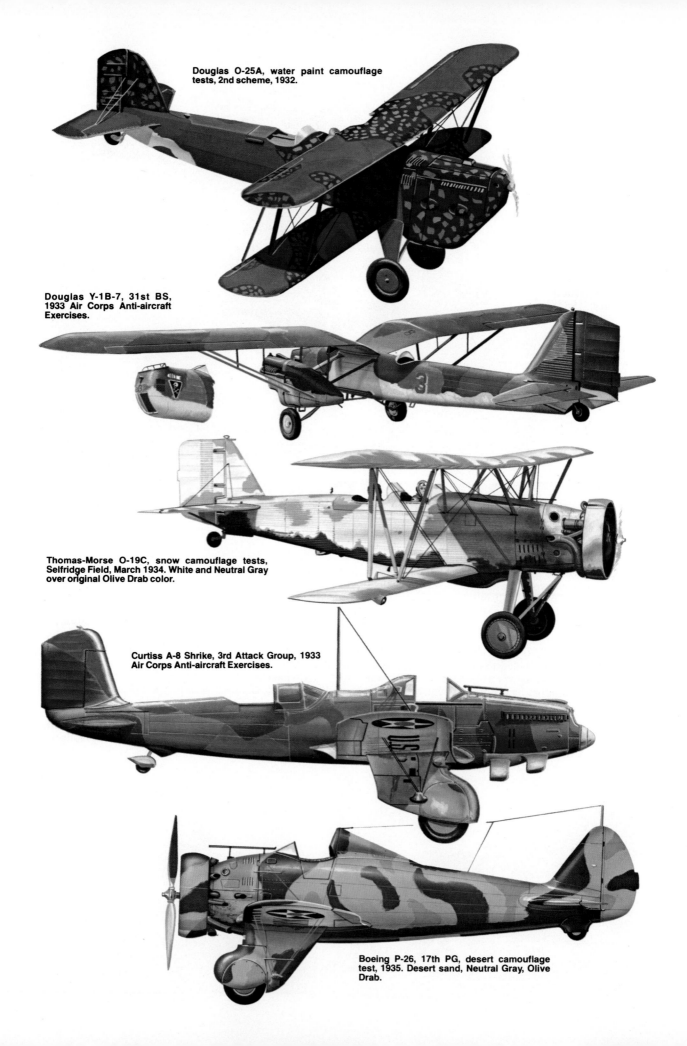

Douglas O-25A, water paint camouflage tests, 2nd scheme, 1932.

Douglas Y-1B-7, 31st BS, 1933 Air Corps Anti-aircraft Exercises.

Thomas-Morse O-19C, snow camouflage tests, Selfridge Field, March 1934. White and Neutral Gray over original Olive Drab color.

Curtiss A-8 Shrike, 3rd Attack Group, 1933 Air Corps Anti-aircraft Exercises.

Boeing P-26, 17th PG, desert camouflage test, 1935. Desert sand, Neutral Gray, Olive Drab.

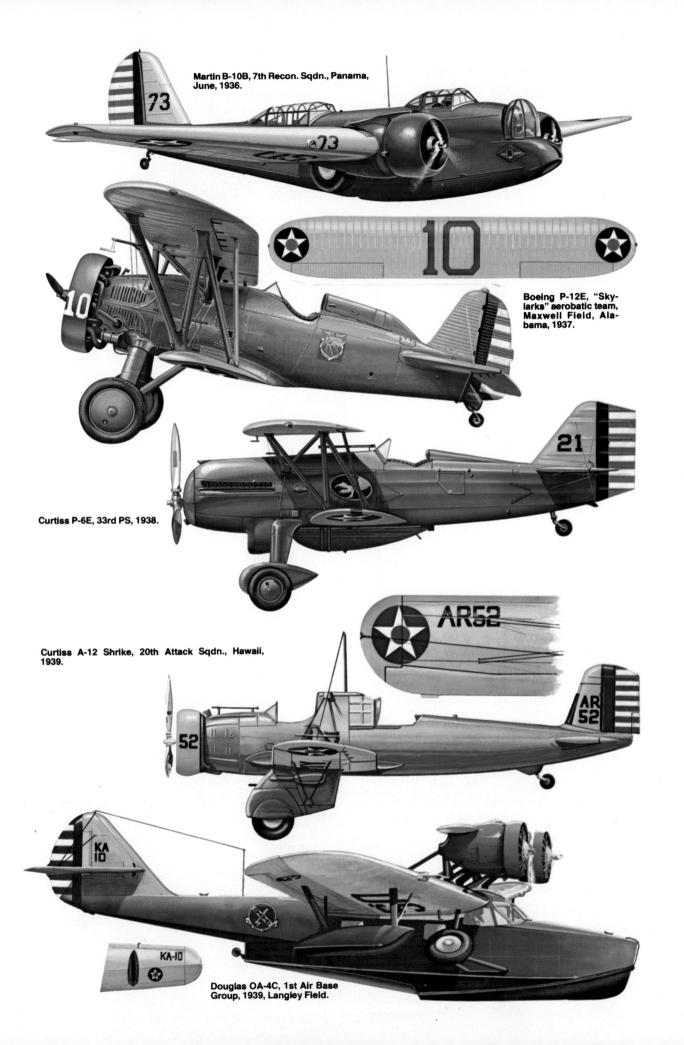

Martin B-10B, 7th Recon. Sqdn., Panama, June, 1936.

Boeing P-12E, "Sky-larks" aerobatic team, Maxwell Field, Alabama, 1937.

Curtiss P-6E, 33rd PS, 1938.

Curtiss A-12 Shrike, 20th Attack Sqdn., Hawaii, 1939.

Douglas OA-4C, 1st Air Base Group, 1939, Langley Field.

Revised designators for reconnaissance aircraft are seen on this 18th Recon. Squadron B-18A during the summer of 1940. The squadron color is apparently red. (USAF)

REVISED DESIGNATORS

ACTIVITY	SYMBOL	EXAMPLE	DESIGNATOR
Air Base	AB	5th Air Base Sq.	5AB1, etc.
Air Depot	AD	Fairfield Air Depot	FAD1, etc.
		Middletown Air Depot	MAD1, etc.
		Southeast Air Depot	SEAD1, etc.
		San Antonio Air Depot	SAAD1, etc.
		Sacramento Air Depot	SAD1, etc.
		Panama Air Depot	PAD1, etc.
		Hawaiian Air Depot	HAD1, etc.
		Philippine Air Depot	PHAD1, etc.
Air Officer	AΘ	2nd Corps Area Air Officer	2AΘ1, etc.
Bomb Group	B	9th Bomb Group	9B1, etc.
Communications Sq.	C	1st Communications Sq.	1C1, etc.
Headquarters	HQ	Headquarters Sq., GHQAF	HQ1, etc.
Instructor (Miscellaneous)	IM	Instructor, Misc.	IM1, etc.
Materiel Division	MD	Materiel Division	MD1, etc.
Miscellaneous	M	4th Comp. Group	4MB1, etc.
National Guard	NG	154th N.G. Obs. Sq.	54 NG1, etc.
Observation	Θ	22nd Obs. Sq. (Air Corps)	22Θ1, etc.
Organized Reserve	ΘR	8th Corps Area Organized Reserve	8ΘR1, etc.
Photo	PH	1st Photo Sq.	1PH1, etc.
Pursuit Group	P	20th Pursuit Group	20P1, etc.
Reconnaisance	R	41st Recon. Sq.	41R1, etc.
School	ED	63rd School Sq.	63ED1, etc.
Staff	S	1st Staff Squadron	1S1, etc.
Technical Supervisor	TS	Technical Supervisor	TS1, etc.
Transport	T	6th Transp. Sq.	6T1, etc.
Wing	W	Headquarters Sq., 2nd Wing	2W1, etc.
Weather (Observation)	WΘ	2nd Weather Obs. Sq.	2WΘ1, etc.

52nd School Squadron BT-14s at Randolph Field in June, 1941. Light Blue fuselages with Orange Yellow wings and tail were still standard for PTs and BTs; note the black anti-glare panels. (USAF)

One of the few early natural metal P-40s was assigned to the Air Corps Technical School's 10th Air Base Squadron. This may be the fifth production airframe, 39-160. (via Cavanagh)

The Materiel Division evaluated new aircraft, such as this B-17C, at its Wright Field facilities. All sections within the Division used the same 'MD' designator. (USAF)

The Neutrality Patrol markings, a star insignia on each side of the nose, are generally associated with the U.S. Navy, but were also carried by GHQAF planes on sea search duties. Shown are 21st Recon Squadron B-18As over Miami in January 1941. (USAF)

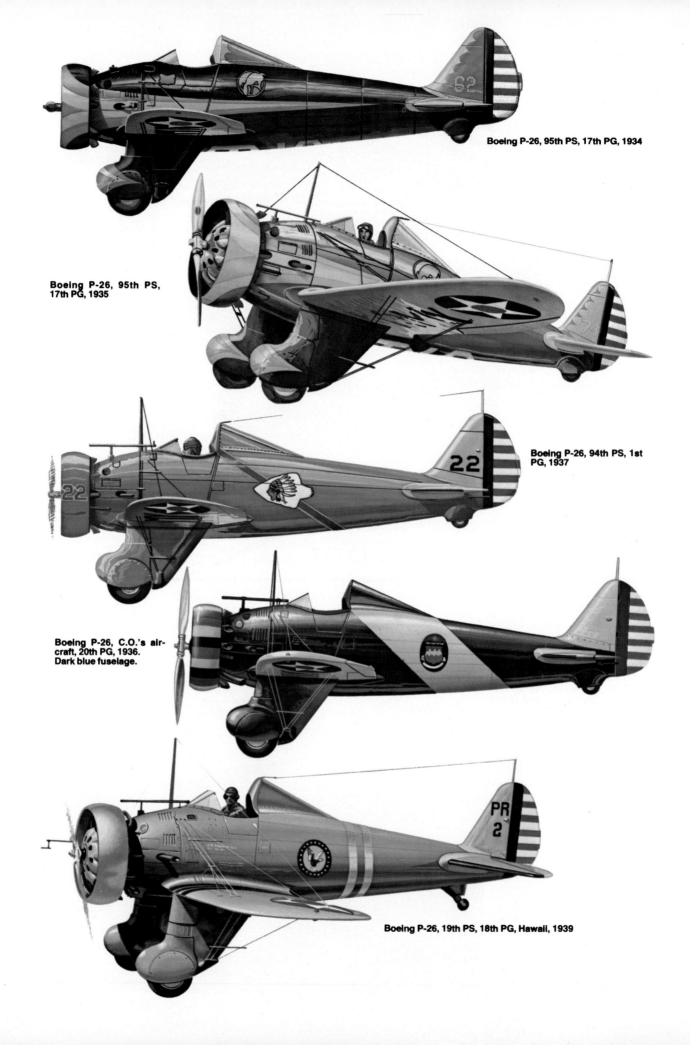

Boeing P-26, 95th PS, 17th PG, 1934

Boeing P-26, 95th PS,
17th PG, 1935

Boeing P-26, 94th PS, 1st
PG, 1937

Boeing P-26, C.O.'s air-
craft, 20th PG, 1936.
Dark blue fuselage.

Boeing P-26, 19th PS, 18th PG, Hawaii, 1939

Forerunner of the AT-6, a North American BC-1A in the markings of the 120th Obs. Squadron, October, 1941. The designator should be 120θ. (USAF)

This aluminum doped P-12E wears the designator of the 5th Corps Area, Organized Reserve, with the insignia of the 308th Obs. Squadron. The small bar through the 'O' prevents this designator from being misread as '50th Recon. Squadron". The individual aircraft number appears on the cowl ring. (Anderson via NASM)

The 17th Pursuit Squadron transferred from the 1st PG to the 4th Composite Group, P.I., in December, 1940. This P-35A wears designators of the new command but most markings have not changed from those worn at Selfridge Field. (AFM via Cavanagh)

A pair of the 1st Photo Group's F-2s over the Alaskan tundra in 1941. The unusual green and orange scheme used by this unit is illustrated on page 65. (USAF)

In November, 1940, the Alaskan Department requested Air Corps permission to repaint the yellow wings and tails of its aircraft with a more orange or red-orange color. The summer yellows of the Alaskan tundra had impeded efforts to locate wrecks, and a different color was considered the solution. Headquarters agreed, and a hue similar to International (not day-glow or fluorescent) Orange became a standard in the region. The pigment had an unfortunate tendency to fade to yellower tones, which revived the original problem, and sometime in 1943, bright Insignia Red was standardized as the high visibility color for Alaska.

The Martin B-10B above has an unusual escalloped design to its orange wing tips and rear fuselage. The photo was taken after a minor landing accident in May 1942. (Mike Monaghan)

One of two B-17Bs of the Cold Weather Test Center, Alaska, photographed in June, 1941. Orange, described as "Mandarin or Chinese" in reports, has been applied to cowlings, wingtips (but not ailerons), and rear fuselage and tail (but not rudders or elevators). By Autumn the color was extended to the control surfaces and a larger area of the wing. (USAF)

Training Colors

In 1927, a young actor named Gary Cooper made his film debut in William Wellman's award winning film *WINGS*. Playing a student pilot, Cooper tossed his Hershey bar on the bunk and walked to his plane to perform "... a few figure-eights before lunch." His subsequent 'death' in a midair collision underscored the dangers of flying, not only to the film's protagonists, but the audience as well.

Cooper's "accident" in *WINGS* was only the beginning of a fine career in motion pictures. But many inexperienced young aviators in the Air Corps training program would not be so fortunate; they stood little chance of surviving an aerial collision. The problem was serious enough that in 1928, the Air Corps began development of a conspicuous color scheme for its trainers. The Olive Drab fuselage then common for most Army aircraft was replaced with Silver dope on a number of Consolidated Primary Trainers and Light Blue on Douglas O-2H's and K's. (Many of the latter planes were redesignated BT-1's when the Basic Trainer category was formed in 1930). Although the methods and results of any comparisons are unknown, Light Blue was adopted for fuselages of all training planes, probably in 1929 or 1930. The Yellow wings that were then standard for other aircraft were also prescribed for all trainers. This basic color scheme would remain unchanged until just before WWII.

In an effort to economize as new, all metal Advanced Trainers were coming into service, the Air Corps decided, in April, 1941, that this type aircraft should have an unpainted aluminum finish. For the time being, PT's and BT's, which were more likely to be fabric covered, and certainly stood a higher likelihood of collision, retained the Light Blue and Yellow scheme.

But not for long! The Air Service Command, which had responsibility for depot maintenance of all aircraft, determined that the absolute minimum overhaul period for a PT-17, the most common Primary Trainer, should be eighteen months, with thirty months being far more desirable. Any shorter period would swamp overhaul facilities, and the Army's accelerated training program would suffer greater shortages of aircraft than could be accepted. Yet, in December, 1941, the life of Yellow doped fabric was only four to ten months. At that time, the only dope with an acceptable service life was Aluminum, and this was applied to all PT-17's produced after March, 1942. (Tech orders did not catch up with the practice until that July, when all trainers became involved).

Dull aluminum was acknowledged to have inferior visibility for training purposes, but the need to train thousands of pilots required a constant supply of training aircraft. The loss of otherwise sound air frames due to fabric deterioration could not be tolerated under the emergency conditions of the first years of World War II. Improved Yellow dopes were soon available, but none could match the durability of aluminum dope.

An interesting sidelight is the emergence of a 'combination scheme' on a number of PT-17's. Several aircraft were flown in blue and yellow colors, with one or more wing sections painted with aluminum! It is not certain if this resulted from mismatching parts during erection of the airframe, or if dope failure of a section resulted in the use of an aluminum doped replacement. This was further confused in the summer of 1942, when rudder striping was eliminated from all aircraft (previously ordered for all combat aircraft by 1 June 1942). Rudders were then to be doped in the same color as the fuselage, and a number of blue rudders were fitted to blue and yellow aircraft.

At the end of August, specifications again caught up with practice, and the rudder striping for all aircraft was formally abolished. At that time, the star insignia was to be added to the fuselage, but many trainers had no room for the marking — their fuselages were covered with large I.D. numbers! Wing insignia continued to be carried in four positions.

This Consolidated PT-3, fitted with leading edge slots, is doped with aluminum fuselage and tail, and yellow wings. Note the absence of wing insignia and markings, relatively common practice for PT-3 aircraft. (USAF)

The PT-3s in this 1931 March Field line up are in O.D. and Yellow. The field I.D. numbers on each fuselage bear no relation to aircraft serials. (via Cavanagh)

Although specifications required blue fuselages on primary and basic trainers, most Ryan trainers such as this YPT-16 were accepted with natural metal fuselages. Wings and tail group are still Orange-Yellow. 1939. (USAF)

FINISH SPECIFICATIONS FOR AIRCRAFT

DATE	PRIMARY & BASIC TRAINERS	ADVANCED TRAINERS	AMPHIBIANS	TACTICAL AIRCRAFT
23 May 1934	Blue & Yellow	Blue & Yellow	Blue & Yellow	Blue & Yellow
24 March 1938	Blue & Yellow	Blue & Yellow	Blue & Yellow	Aluminum
9 Sept. 1938	Blue & Yellow	Aluminum	Blue & Yellow	Aluminum*
20 July 1942	Aluminum	Aluminum	Aluminum	Aluminum*

*Unless camouflage finish applied

Orthochromatic film causes the yellow wings and tail of this Seversky BT-8 to appear darker than the blue fuselage. Thirty of these aircraft, ordered in 1935, were to be the Air Corps' first production monoplane trainers. (R.L. Baseler via Kenn Rust)

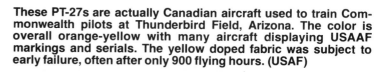

Stearman PT-13As in standard Light Blue and Yellow over Randolph Field, Texas, May, 1938. (USAF)

These PT-27s are actually Canadian aircraft used to train Commonwealth pilots at Thunderbird Field, Arizona. The color is overall orange-yellow with many aircraft displaying USAAF markings and serials. The yellow doped fabric was subject to early failure, often after only 900 flying hours. (USAF)

The second XP-51 during its evaluation period at Wright Field. The designator is repeated on the nose; this repetition was specified for early designators, but not for F.Y. serial call numbers. Spring, 1942. (USAF)

Fiscal Year Designators

The final variation of the radio call number or designator was based entirely on the aircraft serial number. This system, which remains in effect today, appears to have originated with Air Corps Circular 100-4, in August, 1941. Use of the new designator, however, did not become commonplace until 1942.

The numbers were to consist of a minimum of four digits, taken from the last digit of the fiscal year ordered plus the serial number, with as many zeros as necessary to make four digits. Thus, the third aircraft ordered in F.Y. 1941 (an XB-29, serial number 41-3) carried the radio call '1003'; the 18335th aircraft ordered in F.Y. 1941 (another XB-29, s/n 41-18335) was numbered '118335'.

Early tech orders stipulated that a radio call number was to be displayed by each AAF aircraft, but many primary trainers without radios omitted the markings. Also, while camouflaged aircraft were able to use both fin *and* rudder, trainers were to squeeze the digits onto the fin only (since the rudder was covered with red, white, and blue stripes). T.O. 07-1-1 dated 1 June 1942, allowed long designators to appear "on the fuselage" if necessary, though this vague location allowed wide interpretation. Again, there are many examples of this occurring months before the issue of the T.O.

At the same time (early 1942), a new addition was made to field numbers employed by some training bases. A code letter preceded the number to identify the field. In this confused early war period, origins and assigning authorities for these letters are unknown, though their use became widespread later in the war.

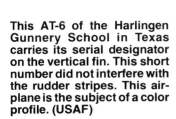

This AT-6 of the Harlingen Gunnery School in Texas carries its serial designator on the vertical fin. This short number did not interfere with the rudder stripes. This airplane is the subject of a color profile. (USAF)

Serials too long for the fin were to be located on the fuselage; this AT-6A carries its radio call number below the cockpit. The field number on the fuselage and cowling uses the base code letter 'T' for Moffett Field. March, 1942. (William T. Larkins)

Camouflage

Much has been written about the Air Corps' temporary camouflage paints, but the truth has long been hidden behind legends and stories. The schemes have long been regarded "faddish," designed and applied with field procured paints which either washed off in the rain or were impossible to remove. Even the popular name "War Games Camouflage" implies that the water paints were designed solely for use in annual maneuvers. Although these stories touch upon the facts, they tend to belie the complex system developed over a period of ten years, a system that was designed to be used if the Air Corps ever went into real battles, not just mock ones.

The "Report on Camouflage of Day Airplanes", published by the Air Services' Engineering Division in January, 1921, set out the precepts and purposes of camouflage that would influence our air force for twenty years. Schemes to decrease an aircraft's visibility when viewed from above were called 'terrestrial camouflage' or 'ground camouflage', and the report suggested that these consist of three-color patterns tailored to fit local terrain colors. Permanent camouflage dopes were prescribed, with additional colored dopes to be added as conditions changed.

One of the major innovations in the study of concealment was 'celestial (or sky) camouflage', to decrease the visibility of aircraft viewed from below. In tests, clear doped aircraft (which had a light yellowish cast) became invisible at an altitude of 17,000 feet. When camouflaged, this altitude was lowered to less than 10,000 feet. It was also found that when so camouflaged, visible aircraft appeared to be flying at higher altitudes, an advantage in confusing anti-aircraft fire.

'Shadow shading' was the subject of some experimentation, with lighter colors being used to reduce shadow areas between wings and beneath the tail. It is a current misconception that the term 'shadow shading' was a reference to a segmented multi-color pattern for upper surfaces, a definition not supported by any reports or correspondence of the period.

The last major recommendation of this 1921 report was that one or both national insignia should be eliminated from the wings of any camouflaged aircraft.

As with any post-war period, military funding was greatly cut in the wake of the Great War. Camouflage in a peacetime air force was a low priority item, and the program was stillborn.

In 1930, the Materiel Division (successor to the Engineering Division) became interested in a temporary means of covering the yellow flying surfaces of aircraft during the annual field maneuvers. A commercial water based paint was ordered in Olive Drab color, and tested on an XCO-8 observation plane. The result was a relatively durable covering which added less than ten pounds weight and cost only $1.25 per airframe. Temporary O.D. was stocked and recommended for use in situations where high visibility colors were undesirable.

The next logical step was to apply camouflage on an aircraft as recommended in the Engineering Division's 1921 report, but using water based temporary paints. This was accomplished in 1932, and a new era of aircraft color schemes followed shortly. For the next three years, aerial surveys of the U.S. recommended new colors and combinations in an effort to standardize colors appropriate over any terrain. These colors were stocked at depots and other facilities, with only a few instances of local purchase of colors. Hues were not normally changed in the field, although paints were occasionally lightened or darkened with black or white. The idea was flexibility: inappropriate schemes could be removed and replaced without building successive layers of paint. A unit moving to a new area could be repainted in a matter of hours. And in peacetimes, the camouflage could quickly be removed after use on maneuvers and exercises.

Removal of the paint required washing in cold water and light scouring with a rag, although there were exceptions to this rule. Certain supplies of Purple and Black paints clung tenaciously to any surface they contacted, but special cleansers were available for their removal.

The use of temporary camouflage was not widespread, and certainly not standard at all 'War Games'. The acceptance of permanent camouflage paints in 1940 brought about the decline of temporary schemes. Water paints saw limited use for altering the O.D. upper surfaces, but the system that had been designed for flexibility over any combat terrain was never put to the test of combat.

After 10 days in the open air, 30 hrs. of flying, and two rainstorms, only a small amount of paint has worn off the elevator and side of the rudder of this XCO-8. Camouflage doctrine of the day included the overpainting of all national markings in an effort to aid concealment. (AFM)

After completion of the tests, one side of the tail was cleaned with cold water and light scrubbing. The finish of the yellow doped tail and red, white and blue rudder was undamaged. (AFM)

Large bands of Olive Drab, Purple, and Dark Green water paints cover this Douglas O-25A during the camouflage experiments of 1932. Sky camouflage was Light blue spotted with White. (NARS)

The same O-25 with smaller sections of each color, and with blotches of OD in Dark Green areas. The undersides were Light Blue with hard edges softened by patches of Purple. This revised scheme was quite satisfactory although small Olive Drab blotches proved unnecessary. (NARS)

The east Virginia landscape has a particularly reddish hue in late autumn. The 2nd BG tested various camouflages on this Y1B-9A (s/n 31-305) to best duplicate the fall terrain at Langley Field. The most effective combination of colors was Dark Green, Purple, a buff (mixed from OD and White), and a reddish-brown (mixed from a locally procured brick color). Undersides are light Blue scalloped with Purple. (AFM)

The Air Corps Anti-Aircraft Exercises in May 1933 offered the first chance to test water based camouflage on a striking force in the field. Pursuits, attack aircraft, bombers and observation planes were painted by generally inexperienced personnel at Patterson Field, Ohio. It took on the average of 6 to 12 man hours per airframe (the massive B-2's requiring 25 man hours each to cover). Ground camouflage colors were identical for all aircraft, being the same Olive Drab, Dark Green, and Purple that had been developed the previous spring. The temporary camouflage was soon popularly known as "War Games Camouflage", and became an irregular feature of maneuvers for the next seven years.

A formation of 31st BS Y1B-7s during the Ft. Knox Anti Aircraft exercises of 1933. (USAF)

This Douglas YlO-43 has an unusually wavy demarkation between the upper and lower colors. Sky camouflage on the manuevers was Light Blue patched with White, although at least one aircraft used purple to break up the lower surfaces. (USAF)

Another Douglas observation design of the early 1930s, this YO-31A sits in the field after a rain. Except for some thinning of the paint on the rudder, the camouflage is intact. Maroon camouflage on the rear of each prop blade was standard in the 1920s and 1930s. (USAF)

A portrait of an 11th BS Curtiss B-2 Condor, with its colorful plumage covered by camouflage. Compare with the view on page 12. (USAF)

A pair of Boeing B-9s taken during the May 1933 manuevers. (USAF via Peter M. Bowers)

Since aircraft at low altitudes could not be effectively hidden from ground gunners, attack ships and pursuits usually did not receive sky camouflage. The orthochromatic film used in this photograph makes this Y1P-16's yellow wings seem much darker. (USAF)

Dark wheel pants made the Curtiss A-8 too visible in flight, so they were repainted Light Blue. The radiator and oil cooler were similarly painted to cover the red squadron color under the nose. (USAF)

One of the three P-6Es on which the 1st PG tested snow camouflage in March, 1934. White water paint was used on upper surfaces and sides, with the wing and tail broken up with patches of aluminum paint. A later test, using an O-19, had better results substituting neutral gray for the aluminum, but neither scheme was particularly effective in sunlight — the shadows were visible even if the aircraft weren't! Snow camouflage saw little use. (AFM)

Probably an early experiment with desert camouflage, this P-12C seems to be painted Dark Green, Olive Drab, Purple and dull red or yellow-orange. May, 1933. (USAF)

In 1934, it was found that Purple paint could not be used for temporary camouflage. In spite of the fact that the color itself was considered valuable, several batches of paint were found to etch metal and crack doped fabric. While new formulas for Purple were tested, Neutral Gray was suggested as a substitute. Although stocks of this color were purchased from manufacturers, Neutral Gray could be mixed in the field from existing supplies of Black and White. Purple was never successfully reformulated, and Neutral Gray became standard from 1935 on.

This 34th PS P-26 was used to develop and test a red-yellow paint that was named Desert Sand. Blotches of Dark Green and Neutral Gray disrupt the outline. This aircraft is illustrated on page 44. (Peter M. Bowers Collection)

A-12s of the 26th AS at Wheeler Field, Hawaii, April, 1937. Colors appear to be combinations of Neutral Gray, Dark Brown, Olive Drab, and Dark Green. (USAF)

P-12s at March Field in November, 1935, apparently painted Desert Sand, Dark Green, and Neutral Gray. Note the camouflaged aircraft number. The wing cocardes on the camouflaged P-12 in the background, right, have not been overpainted, a highly unusual occurrence. (USAF)

The only XP-36B was camouflaged while assigned to Wright Field for testing. The paint job here appears to be particularly uneven, probably OD, Dark Green, and Neutral Gray, with Light Blue below. Note the shadow shading under the stabilizer. (AFM)

Dark Brown paint saw a great deal of use in Hawaii and the Philippines. This O-19 of the 2nd OS appears to be in Dark Brown, Olive Drab, and Dark Green. The aircraft number is camouflaged between the wings, and white on the cowling. January, 1937. (USAF)

Although only a small part of the force involved was camouflaged, the GHQAF Maneuvers of 1938 provided the first large scale test of water soluble paint on natural metal aircraft. As this was a spring exercise, green colors predominated with Dark Blue and Neutral Gray seeing some use. These maneuvers also marked the first known instance of paints being documented by name *and number!* Records of the painting team listed a range (see right) that indicated a new level of standardization had been reached by Materiel Command.

The Colors

25	White	30	Dark Green
26	Sand	31	Dark Olive Drab
27	Light Blue	32	Neutral Gray
28	Sea Green	33	Black
29	Dark Blue	34	Rust Brown

A 7th Bomb Group B-18 is given an early morning coat of camouflage. Citizens of Westfield, Massachusetts reserve judgment as they watch the proceedings. (USAF)

This 20th BS Y1B-17 is probably the only example of its type to be painted a day camouflage scheme. This is BB-52, the subject of our 4 view on page 69. (USAF)

A 31st BS B-18 with flat black water paint for night bombardment. Even with two coats, the metal background shone through in a searchlight's beam. In the May 1938 Maneuvers, five aircraft of the 19th BG were the only B-18s to wear this scheme. (Joe Mizrahi)

Finishing touches for a 95th Attack Squadron A-17A, at Hartford, Conn. Colors are Dark Green, Olive Drab, and Neutral Gray. Maroon paint is chipping from behind the prop. (USAF)

The 95th's A-17As on the line. Ten of these aircraft were camouflaged for the May '38 Maneuvers, and two others are seen in the original natural metal scheme. (AFM)

Four of the 7th BG's five camouflaged B-18s fly formation with an uncamouflaged B-10. The B-18s wear Dark Green, OD, and Neutral Gray on upper surfaces with Light Blue undersides. (USAF)

The 1st PG's Seversky P-35s at the 1938 Fall Anti-Aircraft Maneuvers, Fort Bragg, North Carolina. The colors are probably combinations of Olive Drab, Rust Brown, Neutral Gray and Dark Green. (USAF)

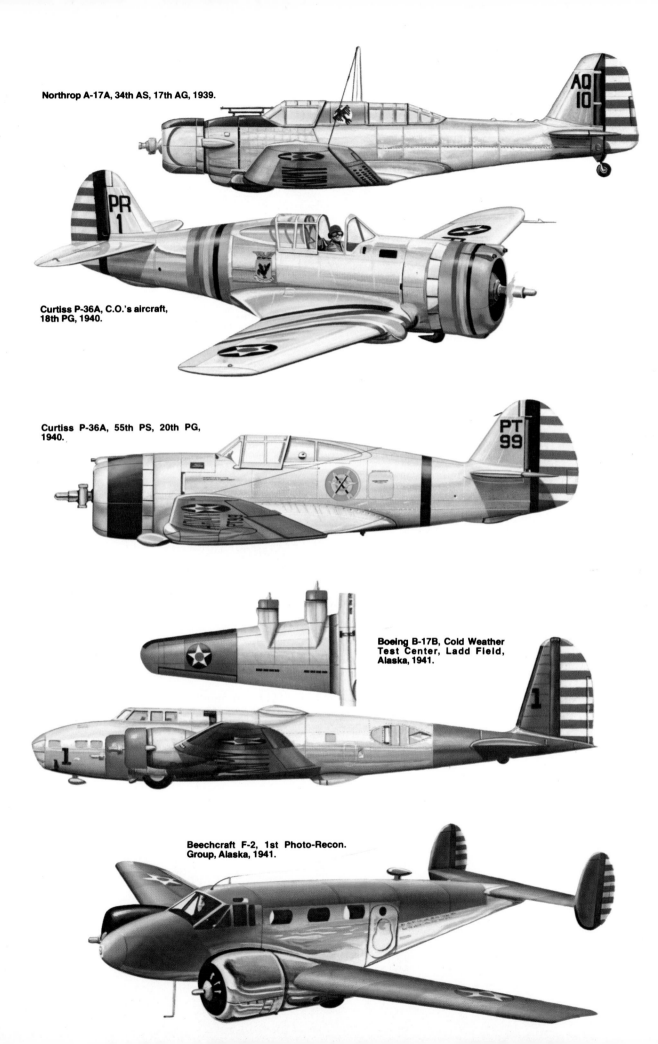

Northrop A-17A, 34th AS, 17th AG, 1939.

Curtiss P-36A, C.O.'s aircraft,
18th PG, 1940.

Curtiss P-36A, 55th PS, 20th PG,
1940.

Boeing B-17B, Cold Weather
Test Center, Ladd Field,
Alaska, 1941.

Beechcraft F-2, 1st Photo-Recon.
Group, Alaska, 1941.

Color numbers 35 through 40 are an unsolved mystery at the time of this writing. The numbers were reserved with QM Corps in January 1939 for paints alleged to be under development, but further documentation has not been found. Even the color names are unknown. The possibility of six unknown colors popping up without notice makes interpretation of any black and white photos in this era a trifle risky. The orange used by the 27th P.S., below, is a prime example, and almost certainly one of the missing six.

These aircraft carry the most famous of the "wargames" camouflage schemes. Ironically, they were painted for the 1939 National Air Races (Cleveland Air Races), and these schemes were never used in any war games or maneuvers. All of these P-36Cs were in the 27th Pursuit Squadron, and no two were painted alike. They provide an interesting contrast to the camouflage schemes carried by European aircraft at the beginning of World War II — the same week. (USAF)

This Curtiss A-18 was one of a number of aircraft painted with elaborate temporary camouflage schemes for a display at Bolling Field, January 1940. Note the smoke generators under the wings. This airplane is the subject of a color profile. (USAF)

This B-17B has been camouflaged with Dark Green, Olive Drab, and Sand above. The under surface color seems particularly light when compared with the Light Blue under the XB-15 in the background. (USAF)

(Above right and right) The Bolling Field Exhibition in January 1940, a chance to show off the Air Corps' new hardware. The XP-36F (toward the left), XP-36E, and XP-36D, as well as the XP-40, XP-39, a YFM-1, a B-18 armed with a cannon and a B-17 appear to use various patterns of Sand, Dark Green, and Olive Drab. Note the differing undersurface colors, perhaps involving Neutral Gray or a newer sky shade. (USAF)

This XA-21 assigned to Wright Field for evaluation is another one-off type at the Bolling Field Air Show. Note the smoke generators mounted on the wing racks. (USAF)

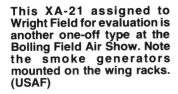

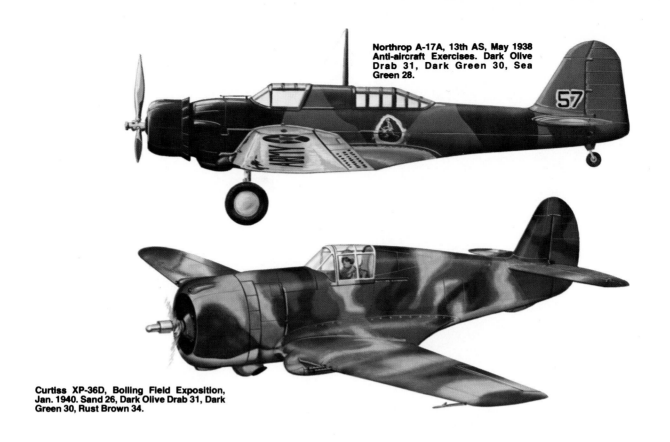

Northrop A-17A, 13th AS, May 1938 Anti-aircraft Exercises. Dark Olive Drab 31, Dark Green 30, Sea Green 28.

Curtiss XP-36D, Bolling Field Exposition, Jan. 1940. Sand 26, Dark Olive Drab 31, Dark Green 30, Rust Brown 34.

Curtiss P-36C, 27th PS, 1st PG, Sept. 1939. (Cleveland) National Air Races.

XP-36F, Bolling Field Exposition, Jan. 1940. Sand 26, Dark Olive Drab 31, Dark Green 30, over Black 33.

Curtiss A-18A, Bolling Field Exposition, Jan. 1940.

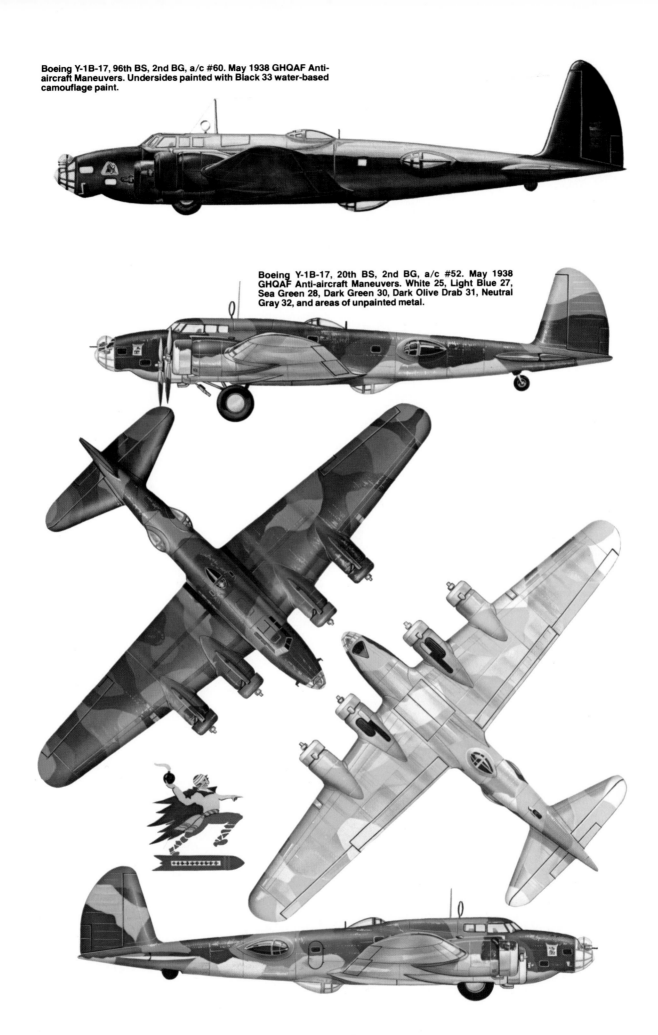

Boeing Y-1B-17, 96th BS, 2nd BG, a/c #60. May 1938 GHQAF Anti-aircraft Maneuvers. Undersides painted with Black 33 water-based camouflage paint.

Boeing Y-1B-17, 20th BS, 2nd BG, a/c #52. May 1938 GHQAF Anti-aircraft Maneuvers. White 25, Light Blue 27, Sea Green 28, Dark Green 30, Dark Olive Drab 31, Neutral Gray 32, and areas of unpainted metal.

The 23rd Composite Group supplied men and aircraft for the Air Corps Board's tests at Maxwell Field. This P-36C was painted OD with Neutral Gray extending up the fuselage sides. Note the glossy cocardes and lack of left upper wing insignia. (Howard Levy via Bowers)

PERMANENT CAMOUFLAGE COLORS 16 September 1940		
41 Dark Olive Drab		45 Insignia Red
42 Medium Green		46 Insignia White
43 Neutral Gray		47 Insignia Blue
44 Black		48 Identification Yellow

Shadow Shading of Aircraft

As noted, the Materiel Division's approach to camouflage was based on temporary paints and schemes being adapted to different background conditions. And yet, when war came, the Army Air Corps was permanently camouflaging its aircraft with only two colors: Olive Drab and Neutral Gray. This drastic shift in policy was largely due to the efforts of Major General H.H. 'Hap' Arnold, Chief of the Air Corps.

In May, 1939, Arnold requested that Materiel Division research factory application of permanent camouflage paint to combat aircraft. The request was ignored, and two months later, Arnold angrily demanded an answer. The Command replied that it still considered "the present water color method" to be the only solution, citing changing background conditions and added cost, weight, and drag of permanent paints. The difficulty finding a paint that adhered to ALCLAD was also explained.

Unconvinced, Arnold pointed out that other powers were purchasing aircraft already camouflaged, and early that August directed that:

1) the Materiel Division experiment with permanent camouflage,
2) demonstration group planes be camouflaged (resulting in the schemes worn by the 27th P.S. at the National Air Races in 1939. See page 66.), and
3) the Air Corps Board at Maxwell Field make a study of various colors and patterns.

The Air Corps Board had originally been activated in August 1937, only to be inactivated the following spring, pending the results of other studies. Arnold's reactivation orders specified that research be directed at "the protective coloring of aircraft in flight and on the ground". Partial reports were required as testing progressed, resulting in most findings being applied long before the final report, "Study #42, The Shadow Shading of Aircraft", was issued in July, 1941.

The recommendation of Dark Olive Drab and Neutral Gray "shadow shading" came early in 1940. Upper surface patterns were found to be of no value, as the colors blended together when viewed from any distance. O.D. adapted to more situations than any other single color, though Dark Green was recommended for predominantly green terrain in summer months. Neutral Gray, used previously to break up Light Blue undersurfaces, was the most satisfactory shade at altitudes above 10,000 feet. The separation of the two colors was to be blended rather than show a distinct demarkation line. (The term "shadow shading" referred to the Neutral Gray countershading of fuselage shadows beneath wings or stabilizers, not to a multi-color upper surface pattern as cited in numerous current publications.) Another major departure from then accepted camouflage doctrine was the display of cocardes — previously, all national insignia had

been omitted on camouflaged aircraft.

General Arnold now had a single color scheme, and in March 1940, he ordered informal negotiations to begin with Curtiss-Wright Corporation. The first Curtiss P-40s were then in advanced stages of assembly, and the Air Corps Chief wanted these aircraft to be delivered ready for combat. Haggling over cost slowed the process somewhat, but with Arnold's personal intervention, all but the first few production P-40s were painted at the factory. Douglas Aircraft Company was also approached, and many early A-20As had camouflage. These early machines, as well as a number of planes camouflaged at depots, can be recognized by the four position wing insignia and full rudder striping. These markings were applied with pre-camouflage glossy paints.

In July 1940, the Air Corps Board's first written memorandum report suggested the removal of one upper and one lower wing star and all rudder striping, proposing the addition of a star insignia to each side of the fuselage. Flat colors were to be used for all insignia. The Board's preliminary findings formed the basis of Specification 24114 issued in late October, 1940. This Spec. gave the Air Corps belated authority to camouflage its aircraft and expect the same from manufacturers.

Initially, unit insignia and markings were unchanged, but as the war loomed closer, the Army instinctively began to remove any colors that detracted from camouflage, or posed a security risk during unit movements.

Designator colors were always specified as yellow. As war approached, many units repainted their designators in black for lower visibility. Many groups and squadrons dropped the designators that identified the unit, leaving only the aircraft numbers. They also eliminated squadron colors, emblems, and command stripes. This was apparently done on a unit-by-unit basis, as no changes had been made in the official specifications except for replacing the old designators with the aircraft serial as a radio call sign. Though effective August 1941, this change was not rigidly followed, many units retaining their old-style designators up to the beginning of the war.

The birth of the U.S. Army Air Force in June, 1941 saw American air power gearing up for war, with airplanes looking ready for the mission.

One serious problem appeared during extended durability tests of the new permanent camouflage colors. On 30 September 1940, the Air Corps Board issued a report complaining about the poor durability of permanent Dark Olive Drab paint. In a test involving three B-12s, after 9 months, all three aircraft showed considerable fading and deterioration. A second test with four B-10s showed slight fading after only two months.

The color usually tended to fade to buff or brown. Later war experiences recorded a wide range of colors when O.D. faded, e.g., from reddish pinks to mousey grays. Because of the urgency in camouflaging a large number of aircraft, the unsatisfactory paint was used pending the formulation of Dark Olive Drab with better weathering characteristics. Thus, planes painted during the early part of the war eventually weathered considerably to a variety of colors depending on local conditions.

Camouflage discipline has had little effect on the markings of these early 55th Pursuit Squadron P-40s. Designators are in yellow rather than black, and the squadron color has been changed from dark blue to white in an effort to *increase* visibility! Note the shadow shading beneath the tails of aircraft numbers 79 and 95. (USAF)

Later recommendations of the Air Corps Board appeared in Specification 24114, revising national insignia, and reducing the contrast of unit markings. Security precautions have brought about the removal of all squadron markings from these 18th PG P-40B's, seen over Hawaii in August, 1941. (USAF)

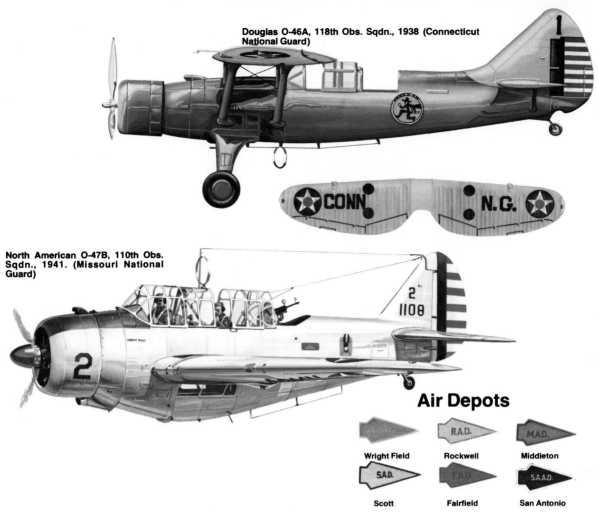

Douglas O-46A, 118th Obs. Sqdn., 1938 (Connecticut National Guard)

North American O-47B, 110th Obs. Sqdn., 1941. (Missouri National Guard)

Air Depots

Wright Field	R.A.D. Rockwell	M.A.D. Middleton
S.A.D. Scott	F.A.D. Fairfield	S.A.A.D. San Antonio

National Guard Squadrons

101st Mass   102nd NY   103rd Penn   104th MD   105th Tenn

106th Al   107th Mich   107th Mich   108th Ill   108th Ill   109th Minn

110th Mo   111th Tex   112th Ohio   112th Ohio   113th Ind   113th Ind

115th Cal   116th Wash   118th Conn   119th NJ   119th NJ   120th Col

120th Col   123rd Ore   124th Iowa   152nd RI   154th Ark

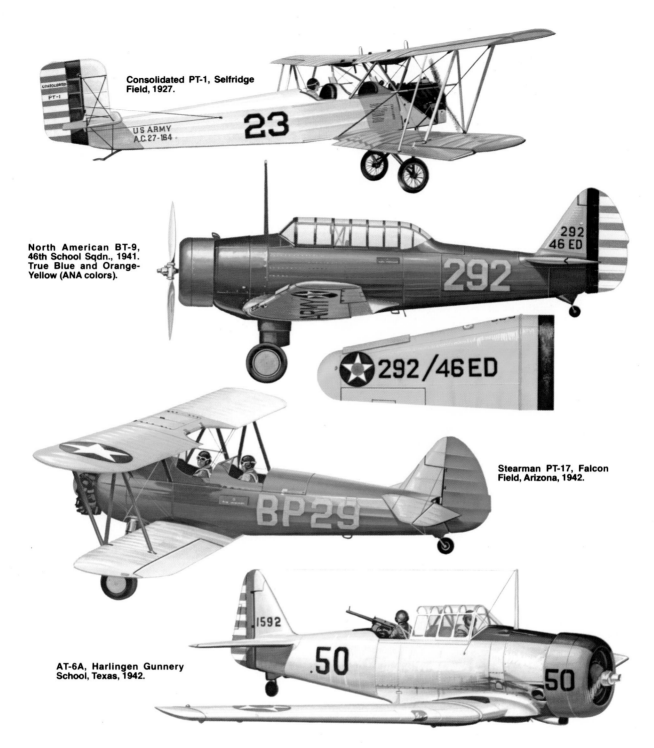

Consolidated PT-1, Selfridge
Field, 1927.

North American BT-9,
46th School Sqdn., 1941.
True Blue and Orange-
Yellow (ANA colors).

Stearman PT-17, Falcon
Field, Arizona, 1942.

AT-6A, Harlingen Gunnery
School, Texas, 1942.

Training Units

46 Sch. Sq.

47 Sch. Sq.

52 Sch. Sq.

53 Sch. Sq.

School of
Av. Medicine

SE Air Corps
Training Ctr.

Gulf Coast
Tr. Ctr.

Air Corps
Tactical Sch.

Air Corps
Tech Sch.

10th Sch. Grp.

11th Sch. Grp.

U.S. Army
Command &
Staff Sch.

Large stocks of OD and Neutral Gray lacquers were not immediately available and water paint camouflage continued to be used well into 1942. Two crewmen are shown applying a temporary finish to a 110th Observation Squadron BC-1A for the Louisiana Maneuvers in August, 1941. Shades are probably Dark Green 30 and OD 31 on upper surfaces. (USAF)

The first A-20As assigned to the 3rd BG were camouflaged with identical patterns of Olive Drab 41 and Medium Green 42, with Neutral Gray lower surfaces. Medium Green 42 was almost identical to the temporary color Dark Green 30. (USAF)

The 8th Pursuit Group refuels at Langley Field in September, 1940. Spec. 24114 would not be issued for another month, leaving these P-40s the only camouflaged aircraft on the field. (USAF)

B-17Cs were built before camouflage orders took effect, so it is likely that this 19th BG Fortress was repainted by a depot. In May, 1941, the 19th began deploying to the Philippines, adding only a plane-in-group number to the tail. (USAF)

Factory applied camouflage covers 31st PG P-39Ds, with unit additions in the form of designators and group insignia. 'U.S. Army' beneath the wing is Insignia Blue 47. (NASM)

The 113th Observation Squadron was Federalized in January 1941, but most of these 0-47s are still wearing Indiana N.G. markings four months later. Only one aircraft carries camouflage, revised national insignia, and the correct designator, '113 Ө1'. (USAF)

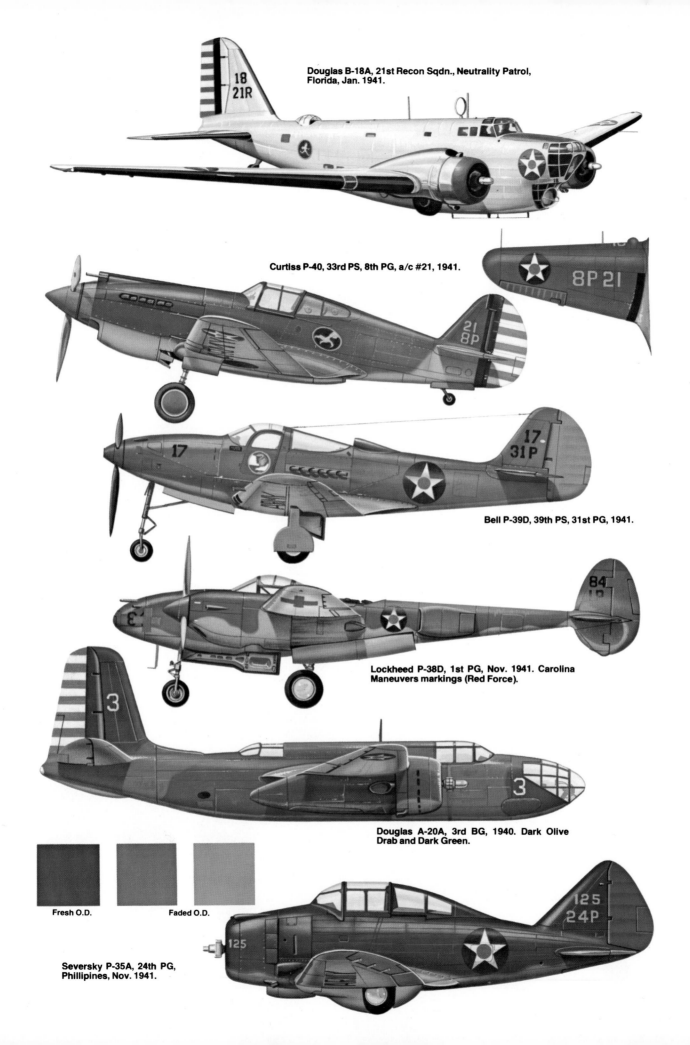

Douglas B-18A, 21st Recon Sqdn., Neutrality Patrol, Florida, Jan. 1941.

Curtiss P-40, 33rd PS, 8th PG, a/c #21, 1941.

Bell P-39D, 39th PS, 31st PG, 1941.

Lockheed P-38D, 1st PG, Nov. 1941. Carolina Maneuvers markings (Red Force).

Douglas A-20A, 3rd BG, 1940. Dark Olive Drab and Dark Green.

Fresh O.D.   Faded O.D.

Seversky P-35A, 24th PG, Phillipines, Nov. 1941.

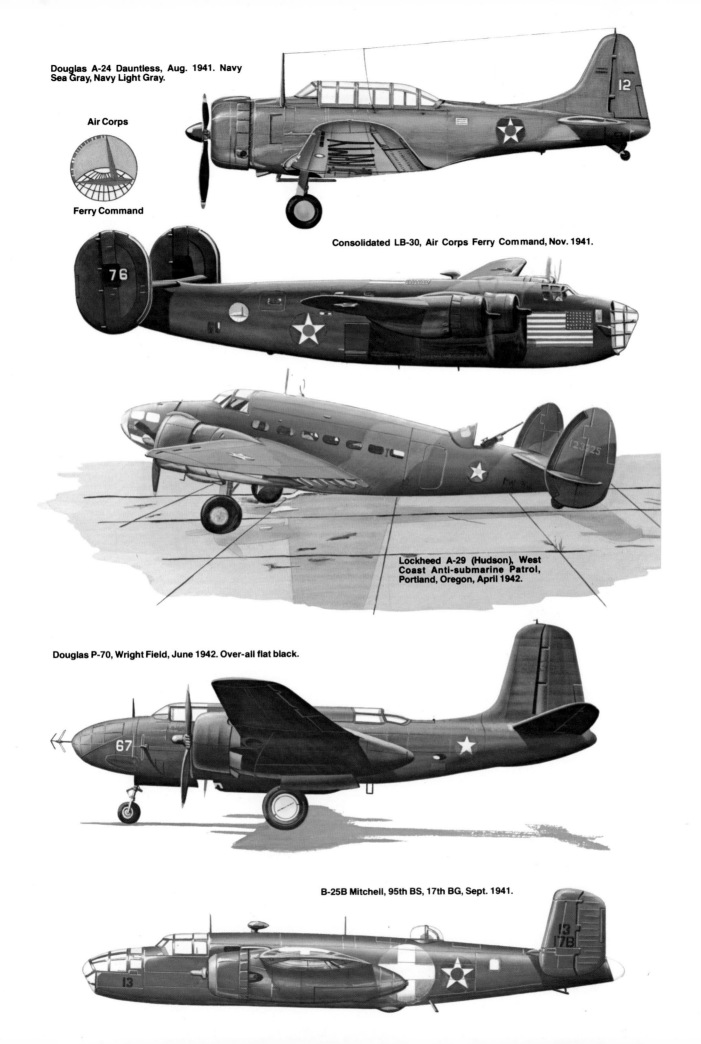

Douglas A-24 Dauntless, Aug. 1941. Navy Sea Gray, Navy Light Gray.

Air Corps

Ferry Command

Consolidated LB-30, Air Corps Ferry Command, Nov. 1941.

Lockheed A-29 (Hudson), West Coast Anti-submarine Patrol, Portland, Oregon, April 1942.

Douglas P-70, Wright Field, June 1942. Over-all flat black.

B-25B Mitchell, 95th BS, 17th BG, Sept. 1941.

This A-20A has its upper surfaces camouflaged in a factory pattern of Olive Drab 41 and Medium Green 42. Markings are for the 33rd School Squadron, assigned to the Air Corps Technical School in the summer of 1941. (USAF)

This camouflage scheme is apparently an attempt at countershading the fuselage sides. Medium Green contrasts strongly with the faded Olive Drab top surfaces and tail of this A-20A of the 58th BS, Oahu, T.H., May, 1941. (USAF)

A Stinson O-49 with water paint 'White Force' markings for the Louisiana Maneuvers in August, 1941. This Vigilant recently switched squadrons, as indicated by the newly painted designator on the tail and original designator (152 Ө 4) above the wing. (USAF)

Although camouflaged and carrying black designators, this P-39D proudly displays the 39th PS's cobra insignia on the cockpit door. The red cross behind the exhaust stacks is a temporary marking during the Louisiana maneuvers in 1941. (USAF)

Even by October, 1941, the weathered OD of this 3rd BG A-20A is shades lighter than the finish of neighboring B-18. White crosses cover the U.S. stars on wings and fuselage during these maneuvers. Props are black without yellow tips. (USAF)

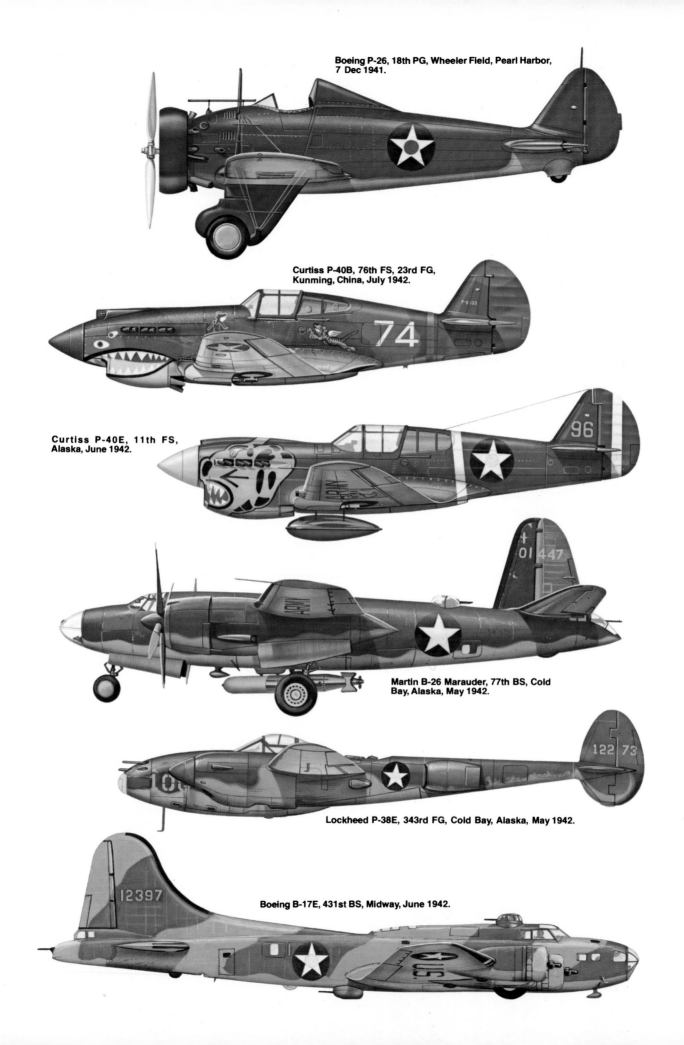

Boeing P-26, 18th PG, Wheeler Field, Pearl Harbor, 7 Dec 1941.

Curtiss P-40B, 76th FS, 23rd FG, Kunming, China, July 1942.

Curtiss P-40E, 11th FS, Alaska, June 1942.

Martin B-26 Marauder, 77th BS, Cold Bay, Alaska, May 1942.

Lockheed P-38E, 343rd FG, Cold Bay, Alaska, May 1942.

Boeing B-17E, 431st BS, Midway, June 1942.

Republic P-43s taxi for take-off during the Carolina Maneuvers in November, 1941. Water paint crosses identify Red Force aircraft. (USAF)

A Douglas C-33 (DC-2) of the 63rd Troop Carrier Group on maneuvers in 1941. The black designator beneath the left wing is noticeably darker than the Insignia Blue used for the word 'Army'. (USAF)

Apparently in an effort to accent the maneuver crosses, these 1st Pursuit Group P-38Ds have had white water paint applied beneath outer wing panels. One aircraft has an inside engine cover applied outside of the engine; the bright oval is a metal mirror that otherwise would allow the pilot to check his nose gear. (USAF)

This well known photo shows one of 12 7th BG Fortresses to arrive during the attack on Pearl Harbor on December 7, 1941. Enroute to the Philippines, these aircraft carried only individual aircraft numbers (in this case #45) for unit identification. (USAF)

In August, 1941, the designator was restructured around the fiscal year serial. The B-26 (40-1503) is wearing the 'radio call' number in November, 1941, although it would be early 1942 before this style of marking would become common. (USAF)

In the aftermath of the Louisiana Maneuvers, these aircraft show the results of numerous attempts to remove 'temporary' water paint markings. The 'White Force' markings have stained the OD camouflage. (USAF)

This B-18 of the 5th BG Headquarters Section was under maintenance when the bombs landed at Hickam Field. Neutral Gray under surfaces tell of incomplete efforts to camouflage the aircraft. (USAF)

The 44th PS at Bellows Field used large plane-in-group numbers in white on the fuselage. Shown is one of the squadron's P-40Cs. (USAF)

Knocked out on the ground, this 18th PG P-40C awaits repair or salvage in the aftermath of the Pearl Harbor attack. (NASM)

Other WW2 Camouflage Colors

Olive Drab and Neutral Gray camouflage, while certainly predominant, was not the exclusive color scheme used on USAAF combat aircraft. The Air Corps Board recommended the use of Medium Green 42 with (or in lieu of) Olive Drab over predominantly green terrain; Sand 26 could be similarly employed over desert areas. However, little use was made of these schemes before June of 1942.

As the 'Arsenal of Democracy', America had been turning out aircraft for foreign governments since 1938. At the time of Pearl Harbor, large numbers of aircraft were awaiting shipment, mostly to the RAF, and numbers of these were repossessed for service with the USAAF. (A Minter Field, California photo taken on 10 December 1941 shows 8 Douglas Bostons dispersed as if ready to repel the expected Japanese invasion. Besides the British camouflage scheme, the aircraft retain their RAF insignia!)

While allocations of aircraft were being juggled to cover rapidly increasing demands, American manufacturers continued to produce aircraft in foreign colors, even though final destinations were uncertain. Many of these aircraft were eventually absorbed by the Army Air Force.

The Joint Aircraft Committee (JAC) was established in September 1940 to coordinate production efforts of the Army, the Navy and the British. One effect of this board was the standardization of camouflage colors, as well as a number of color schemes, in March, 1942. Under this plan, any ship-based aircraft or flying boats would be painted Blue Gray on upper surfaces and Light Gray on under surfaces (U.S.N. colors). Land based planes would be Olive Drab on top and Neutral Gray underneath (USAAF colors). In those cases where aircraft were destined for the Royal Air Force, Olive Drab would be substituted whenever British Dark Green was specified; then, by adding other colors, the basic camouflage could be converted to any desired scheme. This last move was particularly important, as it allowed a single paint to be stocked rather than two similar paints.

Use of the following schemes before June 1942 has been confirmed:

1) The RAF Temperate Day Scheme for fighters and bombers was easily the most common paint job in the USAAF after O.D. and Neutral Gray. American paints were produced to RAF specifications for Dark Earth, Dark Green and Sky Gray (also called "Sky, Type 'S' "), and applied to Tomahawks, Airacobras, Buffaloes, Lightnings, Bostons, Fortresses, Hudsons and so on. Olive Drab was similar enough to RAF Dark Green to be substituted starting in March 1942, when available stocks of Dark Green were exhausted.

2) The RAF Desert Scheme of Dark Earth and Middlestone with Azure Blue under surfaces was primarily an export scheme used on various bombers (Maryland, Baltimore). It was accepted by the USAAF on a number of P-40 Warhawks bound for the North African Theatre.

3) The RAF Night Bomber Scheme was Dark Earth and Dark Green over flat black. A small number of LB-30 Liberators were accepted in these colors before the war, and flown by Ferry Command, with other Liberators impressed early in 1942.

These three schemes were delivered in 'standard' patterns, which were identical on most aircraft. 'Mirror image' versions existed for each pattern, but these reversed schemes were not popular with U.S. manufacturers, and saw limited use.

4) Although the origin of the unusual scheme of Medium Green 42 and Sand (later, Sand 49) over Sky Blue is unknown, its use is documented on Curtiss P-40s, particularly 'E' models. The pattern is identical to that used for the RAF, but the colors need explaining. An OD and Sand scheme was mentioned in tech orders and correspondence, but color slides unquestionably show Medium Green. A grayer under surface color, such as RAF 'Sky' or Neutral Gray 43 might have been logical; Azure Blue (again, RAF) would have been possible — certainly, Curtiss had made use of all three colors for P-40s! However, color transparencies show the under surface a fourth shade, a pastel blue. This color may have evolved as a second U.S. equivalent for 'Sky'.

5) The RAF had discontinued the use of Dark Earth and Dark Green for its day fighters in August, 1941, but American manufacturers were slow to alter their production finishes. The scheme of Olive Drab over Sky was essentially the 'common' parts of the RAF's design, and it was expected that RAF depots would apply Ocean Grey, Middlestone, Dark Earth for bombers, or whatever other color was needed to complete the pattern. There are reports of a deep sky blue used in place of Sky, and this may well be the same under surface color noted on P-40E's above.

The USAAF took possession of a handful of B-24s and B-25s painted in these colors.

6) The standard U.S. Navy scheme of Sea Gray and Light Gray was accepted on A-24s (SBD Dauntlesses) and OA-10s (PBY Catalinas) delivered from Navy production lines. The majority of the Dauntlesses seem to have been repainted with O.D. at a later date.

7) Olive Drab and Neutral Gray could be modified with temporary or permanent paint, depending on which was available. Dark Green 29 (or its lacquer equivalent Medium Green 42) was often applied in non-standard patterns, particularly in Panama. There is no evidence to prove that prior to mid-1942 Green ever replaced O.D. entirely, although this was certainly possible. A number of very early A-20A's were delivered with a standardized pattern of these two colors. The use of Medium Green to break up edges of air-foil surfaces was first ordered in May 1942. When freshly applied, O.D. was

Several LB-30s were accepted in RAF Night Bomber colors for the convenience of production. These served with Ferry Command before U.S. entry into the War, and bore large U.S. flags for neutrality identification. (USAF)

That the Flying Tigers were part of the Chinese Air Force made little difference to the folks back home; they were just as American as the Eagle Squadrons! AVG successes brought good news during hard times. The AVG may have been the first 'American' unit to display kill markings. A 3rd Squadron (Hell's Angels) P-40B, propped up for ground firing tests, shows its Chinese insignia applied over British Dark Earth, Dark Green, and Sky camouflage. The serial number, P-8109, shows this to be one of the first 100 P-40s diverted to China from British orders. (DIA)

darker than the Greens, but the O.D. faded noticeably faster, and usually ended up lighter than Greens applied at the same time.

Several Pacific-based units applied large patterns of Dark Green and Sand to their B-17s, probably adding in any paints left over from pre-war stocks.

8) Two limited schemes for unusual operating conditions were:

flat black, used on a few Douglas P-70 night fighters, and white, used on aircraft in Alaska to cover the high-visibility orange markings. The white may have been a temporary water-based camouflage paint.

This listing is reasonably complete within the first six months of 1942, but the possibility of other color schemes existing in this period is entirely possible, and open to much debate.

Aircraft in war theatres commanded by the Navy often carried Navy-styled markings, such as the red and white rudder stripes ordered in January, 1942. This 5th BG formation is led by a B-17D (40-3064) with two B-17Es (41-2403 and 41-2434). Water based paints are used for two of the aircraft with likely colors being Sand, Medium Green, and Rust Brown. (AAF via Freeman)

One of two XP-51s taken from British Mustang I production and evaluated at Wright Field, in early 1942. RAF Dark Earth, Dark Green and Sky camouflage, with U.S. cocardes in six positions replacing the sixth British roundels. (USAF)

This Lockheed A-29 Hudson wears American equivalents of British Dark Green, Dark Earth, and Sky. British serial BW-454 is beneath the tail in black. (USAF)

Although the upper surfaces pattern of this P-40E is identical to that provided on British Kittyhawks, the colors are Army Air Force Medium Green, and Sand! Lower surfaces are an unidentified light blue. (NASM)

In 1941, a total of 78 Navy SBD-3 Dauntlesses were taken from Douglas production lines and assigned to the 27th BG as A-24s. Deletion of arresting gear, substitution of a larger (pneumatic) tail wheel, and the 'U.S.ARMY' marking beneath the wing were the easiest ways to recognize Army versions — otherwise, these aircraft were identical to their Navy counterparts, right down to the Sea Gray and Light Gray camouflage schemes! Serial numbers, "U.S.Army", and "A-24" were applied to the fin and rudder in small black numbers, similar to the Navy practice. (USAF)

A P-70 night fighter at Wright Field for evaluation in June, 1942, flat black overall, including the nose greenhouse. The first U.S. built night fighters did not see combat until 1943, and then only in limited numbers. (USAF)

This B-25C was built under contract for Britain, but diverted to USAF units. Stars cover the RAF roundels in four wing positions and on the fuselage, but the British fin flash remains. Colors are standard O.D./N.G. (National Archives)

Very little documentation exists of wartime snow camouflage on U.S. aircraft. What little can be seen of this B-18A shows that white has been sprayed over all upper surfaces, including the antiglare panels. The original scheme appears to have been natural metal with orange wing tips. April, 1942. (USAF)

This UC-64 has a coat of white over everything except the national markings and the orange paint beneath the wings and stabilizer. White snow camouflage does not appear to have been used by the USAAF after the winter of 1941/42. The crewman in front of the windscreen may have found the only warm spot for miles! (USAF)

The 28th Composite Group moved to Alaska in February, 1941. These P-36As, photographed in April, 1942, retain four position wing insignia and rudder striping, with no fuselage stars; this was a full year and a half after the directives had changed these markings for camouflaged aircraft. (USAF)

This 22nd BG B-26 was photographed at Hammer Field, California prior to deployment to the Philippines in spring 1942. The dragon insignia of the 33rd BS was probably removed before the beginning of the trans-Pacific flight as a security move. (USAF)

The simple markings of the Doolittle Raid B-25s were not unlike those of most USAAF aircraft in April, 1942: factory applied! The only additions are occasional plane-in-group numbers or personal devices on the nose. (USAF)

One of the Doolittle B-25s soars down the flight deck of the USS Hornet. The Olive Drab upper surfaces appear to have been touched up in several places. (USAF)

One of the problems faced by every combatant air force has always been the rapid identification of friendly vs. enemy aircraft during the action of a battle. Accurate aircraft recognition during the Second World War was no exception, with inadequate training, poor visibility, or confusion of the moment being contributing factors. The man behind the gunsight (whether ground based or aerial) needed immediate clues to an aircraft's identity and intent, and often it became a case of shoot first and ask questions later. This was true as early as 7 December 1941, when American anti-aircraft guns in Hawaii opened fire on "the second wave" at 11:00, well over an hour after the last Japanese aircraft had left the scene. Similar confusion resulted at Clark Field in the Philippines when approaching Japanese fighters were mistakenly identified as P-40's; many ground crews who left the safety of their shelters were subsequently strafed.

In the Pacific, this often stemmed from the red center of the US (also British) national insignia being mistaken for the Japanese Hinomaru. The flash of red in the sunlight could easily bring a hail of 'friendly' fire. At an unknown date in the spring of 1942, Far Eastern Air Force units began overpainting the center of the star with white. On 12 May 1942, the Combined Chiefs of Staff ordered the removal of the red circle and the red and white rudder stripes (by then used primarily by the Navy) from all US COMBAT aircraft after 15 May. On 28 May, Spec 98-24102 was similarly revised, but on 1 June, T/O 07-1-1 ordered removal of the red for all aircraft, training or other-

wise. Orders deleting the red, white, and blue rudder stripes from trainers were not published until late August, though the practice had been noted as early as June.

It is important to note that these changes required removal of the red markings, not simply the discontinuance. The change was not expected to wait for the next depot overhaul, but was required of all units, especially those in the field. While some photos dated July and August 1942 show the "meatball" center intact, compliance with these directives was generally accomplished quickly.

In April 1942, several manufacturers requested permission to omit the "U.S. ARMY" marking being painted beneath the wings of combat aircraft. They hoped to conserve paint and man hours, and some questioned the validity of putting such identification markings on aircraft that were allegedly invisible anyway! An agreement with the Materiel Division appears to have been reached by early May, and many aircraft appeared without the marking shortly afterward. Similar deletions for trainers were published on 2 November, but there are examples of training aircraft without the "U.S. ARMY" wing marking appearing the previous summer.

The omission of the underwing identification marking was basically an economy move, and no orders were cut prescribing the removal of the marking for aircraft already in service. Even in 1945, there were a number of older aircraft which continued to display the label.

Two Randolph Field Aviation cadets watch as white paint is sprayed over the red center of an insignia. White overspray extends into the blue circle. (USAF)

A heavily weathered P-39D at a U.S. training base in 1942. Note the 'ghosts' of the red center within the white stars. Masking tape seals the radio compartment door aft of the fuselage insignia. (USAF)

Reinforcements for The Flying Tigers, these P-40Es cross the Atlantic on board the aircraft carrier U.S.S. Ranger. A brush and white paint cover the insignia's red center, June, 1942. (National Archives)

On the morning of 20 February 1942, seven 19th BG B-17Es attacked Japanese ships off the coast of Bali. Upon returning to Malang, they were in turn strafed by Japanese fighters, which destroyed three of the Fortresses (including 41-2488, shown here), and damaged two others. (via Tagaya)

The first USAAF combat unit to adopt an outlandish unit marking during WW II was the 11th F.S. in May, 1942. The grotesque yellow "Aleutian Tiger" nose markings are usually credited to Squadron Commander Lt. Col. John S. Chennault, son of Flying Tigers leader Clair Chennault. The white fuselage stripe may have been an early marking for all Allied fighters in Alaska, with the single tail stripe further identifying the 11th F.S. (USAF)

The nose emblem of this Aleutian P-40E appears to be a mosquito dive-bombing over an Alaskan mountain range. This may have been an unofficial insiginia of the 11th FS, May, 1942. (NARS)

The desperate situation in the Netherlands East Indies led to the 5th Air Force's use of a number of unlikely aircraft. This export version of the Brewster Buffalo, originally intended for the Dutch, was taken over in early 1942. The colors are probably Foliage Green, Earth Brown, and Sky, all from Australian paint stocks. (Peter Malone via Jim Maas)

This Lockheed A-29 (Hudson) was photographed in Portland, Oregon, April 1942. This plane, assigned to anti-submarine patrol duty, was originally produced for the R.A.F., and impressed into American service. The British serial "BW-463" is barely visible under the tail. (USAF)

Reinforcements arrive after the Battle of Midway. These 73rd FS P-40Es carry a two toned pattern of OD and Medium Green, with Neutral Gray undersurfaces. Four wing insignia are carried to conform with Navy practices in the theater. "Flagship Mary Ann" wears the plane-in-group number '100' on its fin. (NARS via Cressman)

B-17Es of the 431st BS wore a variety of schemes during the Battle of Midway. This aircraft has its OD uppersurfaces broken up with a pattern of Sand and Dark Green. (USAF)

This P-40B of the 76th FS, 23rd FG, in China, July 1942, still carries AVG markings although U.S. insignia have been painted over the original Chinese markings. (USAF)

As war came to the Philippines, the 28th Bomb Squadron was the only unit maintaining combat ready B-18s, and none of these flew operational sorties. When the Japanese arrived at Clark Field in the spring of 1942, this B-18 was relatively intact, and still wearing OD/Neutral Gray camouflage. The sole unit marking is a yellow aircraft number (5) on the fin. (Koku Asahi via Tagaya)

The Colors

First issued in 1919, Quartermaster Corps Spec. 3-1 was the standard for Army paints until 1943. As originally published, the specification included a color card with 24 paint samples; the later camouflage colors were sent to the QM Corps for approval, and carried consecutive numbers, but were never added to the color card. Air Corps Bulletins were printed and circulated with these samples.

To complicate matters, a number of other specifications were employed by the Air Service, Air Corps, and Air Force, and it is likely that supplies from different specs could be found in the same stockroom on any given date. An Ultramarine Blue and Venetian Red were in use for national insignia through most of the 20's, but the origin and

authority for this paint remain a mystery to this date. In 1934, the Air Corps began circulating sets of its own porcelain enamel color plates, separate from the 3-1 colors, but use of these standards appears to have been short-lived.

Throughout the '20s and '30s, the Air Corps and the Navy had maintained separate and unrelated standards for colors. Although both services used red, white and blue insignia, and painted their wings a high visibility yellow, the colors were distinctly different, even to the casual observer. By 1939, agreement was reached on a single "Army-Navy Aircraft" standard for all peacetime colors; paints remaining in stock continued to be used until depleted. It was not until August, 1942 that camouflage colors were brought under similar control.

The following notes will point out the variations of basic colors under the separate specs, as seen on surviving color cards. Color shifts from exposure to the elements and staining produced further changes under service conditions.

LIGHT BLUE: The "standard" fuselage color was shown on 3-1 sample #23. The Air Corps color plates showed a darker, purpler, and stronger color. Navy 'True Blue' was the accepted color under ANA standards, and this was lighter, much stronger, and slightly purpler than the Air Corps color.

YELLOW: The high visibility color used for wings and tails was #4 on QM Spec 3-1. The Air Corps color was lighter, greener, and stronger. With ANA standards, Navy "Orange Yellow" was adopted by both services, but in reality this color was not as orange as either the QM or the Air Corps color. It was, in fact, yellower, lighter, stronger, and slightly greener than the Air Corps sample. None of the colors was ever known as "Chrome Yellow" under American standards.

RED (insignia): No color plate exists of the bright red used during the 20's, although existence of the color can be confirmed from contemporary oil paintings, produced by engineers documenting camouflage schemes. The Spec 3-1 color was #15, but the Air Corps color plate was actually closer to #16 Vermillion, being darker, purpler, and weaker than #15. Again, the Navy insignia color was standardized under ANA,

and this was lighter, yellower, and stronger than the Air Corps color. For camouflaged aircraft, Insignia Red 45 was a flat version of the ANA spec color. A dull red based on the British insignia color was approved as the ANA standard in 1942, but by this time, red was no longer used in the US insignia.

BLUE (insignia): As with the early red, samples of the blue insignia color of the 20's have not been located. Spec 3-1 color #24 was prescribed, but the Air Corps plates were darker, stronger, and a little purpler. The Navy insignia blue was the basis for the ANA color, and was much lighter, stronger, and purpler than the Air Corps plate.

OLIVE DRAB: QM Spec color #22 was a good match for Air Corps OD, though the latter was a bit lighter, a little stronger, and a slight bit yellower. The ANA spec was the same as the 3-1 color, but the Navy made little use of Olive Drab in any case. The camouflage color was Dark Olive Drab (#31 or #41) which was darker and greener, but the word 'Dark' was rarely used, and was dropped in June 1943.

The above color comparisons were made to surviving samples of original Paint specifications and the current Federal Specification 595a. None of these represents a systematic approach to color values; all are collections of paints in use. Relations between colors were made with a critical eye under daylight conditions, with comments to relate the vintage color to the closest FS 595a equivalent.

Color Comparisons with F.S. 595a

No.	Color	F.S. equiv.	Notes
1	*Ivory Cream*	13596	#1 is a little lighter, stronger, yellower
2	*Colonial Yellow*	13596	#2 is darker, stronger, slightly redder
3	*Buff*	10371	#3 is slightly lighter, and stronger
4	Yellow	13432	#4 is darker, yellower, and weaker
5	*Orange Yellow*	11302	#5 is a little more orange, a little lighter, and a little stronger
6	*Light Green*	34524	#6 is lighter, yellower, a little stronger, and glossy
7	*Green*	14090	#7 is yellower and darker
8	Olive Green	34098	fairly good match; #8 is stronger, a little yellower, and glossy
9	*Bronze Green*	14050	#9 is a little darker, glossy
10	*Light Gray*	16357	#10 is glossier, darker, yellower, stronger
11	*Warm Gray*	16555	#11 is glossier, a little darker, a little yellower, a little stronger
12	*Blue Gray*	36307	#12 is glossy, darker, and yellower
13	*Dark Gray*	36081	#13 is glossy, stronger, browner
14	*Pink*	10371	not a good match; #14 is glossier, lighter, stronger
15	Flag Red	11105	#15 is glossier, a bit lighter, a bit stronger
16	*Vermilion*	11136	#16 is glossier, darker, a little stronger
17	*Metallic Red*	20152	#17 is glossy, a little darker, much stronger, yellower
18	Maroon	10076	poor match; #18 is glossier, yellower, stronger, a bit lighter
19	*Seal Brown*	30108	#19 is glossy, stronger, and slightly lighter
20	*Brown Primer*	20122	#20 is glossier, lighter, stronger, a bit redder
21	*Warm Drab*	26134	#21 is glossier, a bit darker, a bit stronger
22	Olive Drab	30118	#22 is glossy, stronger, darker, a bit redder
23	Light Blue	35109	poor match, #23 is stronger, a little greener, a little lighter, glossy
24	Flag Blue	15044	#24 is glossier, darker, a little stronger

The colors in italics existed, but their use on aircraft cannot be confirmed.

No.	Color	F.S. equiv.	Notes
25	White	37778	#25 yellows with age, probably closer to 37886 originally
26	Sand	30279	#26 is slightly darker and pinker
27	Light Blue	35622	poor match; #27 is much darker and deeper blue
28	Sea Green	34128	#28 is less yellow and greener
29	Dark Blue	none	#29 is about halfway between 35109 and 35189
30	Dark Green	34092	#30 is slightly blacker
31	Dark Olive Drab	34087	good match
32	Neutral Gray	36173	#32 is very slightly darker and neutral in color
33	Black	37038	
34	Rust Brown	30117	#34 is slightly darker

Colors 35–40 are not known at this time.

No.	Color	F.S. equiv.	Notes
41	Dark Olive Drab	34087	#41 is slightly redder and tends toward 34086
42	Medium Green	34092	good match
43	Neutral Gray	36173	#43 is neutral in color
44	Black	37038	
45	Insignia Red	31136	good match
46	Insignia White	37855	#46 was probably closer to 37886 originally
47	Insignia Blue	35042	#47 is lighter and bluer
48	Identification Yellow	33538	#48 is darker but same hue; not as dark as 13432

Other Comparisons

Water paint test of July 1930

Olive Drab	30118	sample is slightly darker and very slightly greener

Color samples attached to report of 22 January 1932

Olive Drab	30118	good match, with sample slightly lighter and slightly greener. One sample is close to 30266, but slightly darker
Purple	37144	very poor match, with the sample being bluer and lighter, more of a 'Royal Purple'
Dark Green	34108	good match, with some samples being darker and some being lighter. One sample was close to 34128

Camouflage report of 10 August 1932

Olive Drab	34087	sample is slightly greener
Purple	37144	poor match; sample is richer and darker
Dark Green	14036	sample is flat; redder

These P-40s of the 23rd Fighter Group in China in mid-1942 still carry RAF-style camouflage and the "shark mouth" markings carried by AVG (Flying Tiger) aircraft. Most of the AVG planes survived for many months in their original paint schemes, a few even in Chinese markings. In most cases of repainting, U.S. insignia were painted over the Chinese markings, but little else was altered. (NARS)

MIG KILLERS

...AND KILL MIGS

By LOU DRENDEL

$6.95

squadron/signal p...

MIG ALLEY

by Larry Davis

$7.95

6020

1170

squadron/signal publications